THE VISUAL PREACHER

"*The Visual Preacher* offers encouragement and concrete tips to preachers who are ready to embrace and enhance the visual aspects of proclaiming the good news. Even for those preachers who are not convinced pandemic-induced online preaching is here to stay in one form or another, the book offers guidance for studying the Bible visually, utilizing images and video, and crafting sermons for people who wish to *see* Jesus."

—Shauna K. Hannan, professor of homiletics, Pacific Lutheran Theological Seminary, and core doctoral faculty member, Graduate Theological Union, Berkeley, California

"I've been a fan of Steve Thomason's *Cartoonist's Guide to the Bible* for many years. Now he shows us how we, too, can become visual preachers—even if you're artistically challenged like me!"

—Robert Williamson Jr., professor of religious studies, Hendrix College; author of *The Forgotten Books of the Bible: Recovering the Five Scrolls for Today* (Fortress Press, 2018); cohost of *BibleWorm* podcast

"Wow! I wish you could see me offer that exclamation in person, because the printed word doesn't capture my amazement at what Steve Thomason has accomplished with *The Visual Preacher*. Chock-full of much-needed, practical wisdom from a seasoned preacher, artist extraordinaire, and communication guru, Thomason's book offers the church an incredible and timely gift for all who proclaim the gospel. This little gem is a must for any preacher today."

—Jason Brian Santos, Community Presbyterian Church, Lake City, Colorado

THE VISUAL PREACHER

*Proclaiming an
Embodied Word*

STEVE THOMASON

Fortress Press
Minneapolis

THE VISUAL PREACHER
Proclaiming an Embodied Word

Cover design: Alisha Lofgren / Tory Herman / Kristin Miller

Print ISBN: 978-1-5064-6473-2
eBook ISBN: 978-1-5064-6474-9

To my dad. You helped me see Jesus.

CONTENTS

ILLUSTRATIONS

ACKNOWLEDGMENTS

So many people have contributed to this book in various ways. Allow me to name them and love on them, just a little.

First, I am thankful for the various congregations I have served over the years that have allowed me to experiment—and obsess—over the use of visuals in preaching. Thanks to Central Christian, where I cut my teeth as a preacher; to Hart Haus, where *A Cartoonist's Guide to the Bible* was born; to Grace Lutheran, which welcomed me into the Lutheran tribe; and to my current congregation, Easter Lutheran, which has allowed my visual preaching style to grow and thrive.

Many colleagues have walked with me along this journey and cheered me on. I couldn't have done this without the many coffee meetings with Terri Elton, the nudge to get the iPad from Michael Binder, or the constant encouragement to express complex theological constructs in my own visual fashion from Mary Hess.

I am grateful for the colleagues who were willing to spend an hour or so with me on Zoom to record the Visual Preacher Interview series: Dan Currell, Paul Oman, Stephanie Williams O'Brien, Rolf Jacobson, Karoline Lewis, Cyndee Buck, Mary Hess, Keith Anderson, and Shauna Hannan. You taught me so much about visual communication.

I am deeply grateful for the team at Working Preacher and my editor, Beth Gaede, and publisher, Will Bergkamp, for their encouragement and collaborative creativity. From the moment Beth reached out to me with the invitation to write this book, she has been a source of positive energy that has gotten me through some tough moments of writer's block and self-doubt. Thanks to Will for giving me grace when the pandemic and a lot of uncertainty in our congregation made it difficult to focus. Thanks to the Working Preacher team for thinking I could be the one to write a book about "preaching for the eye."

Above all, I am thankful for my family, who has put up with this crazy cartoonist/pastor for a really long time. My kids still think my drawings are fun, even though they are all adults. My parents have encouraged my art and preaching since I was in grade school and still help me process my sticking points weekly over coffee. Finally, I am so thankful for my wife, Lona, who never gives up on me, even when I'm ready to throw in the towel.

All of you have helped me see Jesus. I hope this book will help others see Jesus a little more clearly too.

INTRODUCTION

Visual preaching is in my blood. It started with my father. He first encountered the good news of Jesus as a high school student in the 1950s and imprinted on the gospel within an independent Baptist church in a first-ring suburb of Detroit, Michigan. He was interested in art and ministry. A book titled *Your Chalk Can Talk* by George Sweeting captured his imagination. The book showed him how to construct a large easel, equipped with ultraviolet lights on a rheostat, upon which he could draw large images with chalk in a public space.

This is how his visual preaching began. He purchased a reel-to-reel tape recorder and convinced the church organist to record half an hour of music for him. He spent much of his young adulthood standing in front of congregations, drawing beautiful images, wowing people with the black light and fluorescent chalk effects, and proclaiming the gospel.

Visual communication is genetic for me, you see.

My art career began when I was in fourth grade. That's when I knew that my drawing skills were special and I would be an artist. My dad saw the gift and fanned the flames. He gave me every book on art that he had collected as a young man. Included in that stack was, you guessed it, *Your Chalk Can Talk*. He was no longer doing chalk talks by the time I came along. Yet when he told me the stories of his chalk talks, I was hooked and dreamed of doing them myself.

It is in my blood.

Blame It on Bruce

While my love for visual communication is genetic, to be sure, I really need to blame Bruce for igniting my desire to become a visual communicator of the gospel and offering me a firsthand experience of its power. Bruce Wilkinson created an organization called Walk Thru the Bible in the 1970s. He came to our church when I was in sixth grade, and he changed my life.

It was a Saturday morning. We had set aside the whole day for this event. The church sanctuary sat one thousand people, and the place was packed. Bruce stood before us with a massive screen and an overhead projector. He placed a full-color image on the projector, and I was transfixed. Then he invited the audience to become a living map. He designated different sections of the audience to play different parts of the map, as if it were laid out over the crowd and we were inside it. Each region of the map had a different hand motion or sound that designated it as a particular geographical location in the biblical world: the Mediterranean Sea section would wave their hands back and forth over their heads to show they were the sea, the desert region would place their hands on their foreheads and moan as if they were extremely parched, and so on. He moved into the crowd, through the various regions we had been assigned, and literally walked us through the story of the Hebrew Bible. He then talked through the major points of the biblical narrative by associating each one with a key word, a cartoon image, and a hand motion. For example, the first event was creation. He instructed each of us to put our hands together in front of our waist and then raise up both arms on each side of our body until our hands met at the top. This movement formed a big circle. As we made this movement, we said, "Creation." By the end of the day, we could tell the story with key words and hand motions: "Creation, Fall, Flood, Nations. . . ." These mnemonic and kinesthetic devices helped glue the biblical narrative to our memory.

I was already a Bible nerd and an artist as a sixth grader, so Bruce's presentation that day was like pouring gasoline on a fire. I was hooked. From that moment forward, I wanted to dedicate my life to using art and visual communication to proclaim the gospel of Jesus and draw people (pun intended) in to a deeper understanding of God and Scripture.

So you see, I blame it on Bruce.

Beginning the Work

I emerged into young adulthood in the 1980s, when evangelicalism was a progressive movement of wonder and questions and the visual communication industry in Hollywood was being transformed by creators like George Lucas and Steven Spielberg. I graduated from Wheaton College with a degree in art, emphasizing in film and animation, at the same time that the Walt Disney Company was unfolding the dawn of a new golden age of animation. I was obsessed with animation. Everything in my life was about visual communication, a sense of wonder at God's creation, and mastering the skills of art and biblical teaching.

My plan was for God to allow me to become a Disney animator so that one day I could open my own animation studio. I wanted to open the studio in the inner city and help kids there find a way to hone their art skills. I wanted to create amazing educational animations to ignite the world's interest in God and Scripture.

It turns out that we don't get to make God's plans for our lives. God chose other people to live out that dream. Now I get to watch the folks at BibleProject do it better than I ever could have imagined.

God closed the door on my dreams to become a Disney animator and opened the doors for me to come on staff at a church in Las Vegas. This church was the third congregation to join the Willow Creek Association. We were early adopters and innovators in the evangelical megachurch movement of the 1990s. Vegas was booming. The church was growing like wildfire, and I was one of the preachers.

There I was, a twentysomething artist-preacher at a church that valued innovation and experimentation among its highest virtues. I preached my first sermon in 1994. I stood up in front of the congregation to preach. Guess what I brought with me? An overhead projector. Thanks, Bruce.

I preached this sermon during a time when my full-time job was managing the caricature and airbrushed T-shirt businesses in multiple hotels/casinos on the Las Vegas Strip. I had access to a top-of-the-line color laser printer. This allowed me to take full-color images that I had painted on paper, scan them, and print them on overhead transparency film for use in my sermon.

That first sermon brought my two worlds—art and preaching—together. The text was the story of Elijah as he confronted the prophets of Baal and then ran for his life. Elijah's taunting of the prophets made me think of Arnold Schwarzenegger (who was just breaking into movies at the time). So I drew a caricature of Elijah as Arnold and scanned it onto the overhead transparency film.

The congregation seemed a little uneasy as they saw the overhead projector sitting there by the pulpit. My first few transparencies were full-color maps of the Holy Land, upon which I drew circles and arrows to demonstrate where the events of the text took place.

No one seemed impressed. Where was the fascination that I felt that day as a sixth grader when Bruce mesmerized me with his projected maps?

I started to panic-sweat.

Then I started telling the story of Elijah on the mountain: "The prophets of Baal worked all day, calling out to their god to bring the fire."

Then it happened.

I placed the full-color caricature of Elijah as Arnold on the projector. In my best Arnie impersonation, I taunted the prophets, "Shout louder, maybe your god is sleeping."

The congregation burst into laughter. My career as a visual preacher was launched.

I worked at that church from 1994 to 2002 while I earned an MDiv from Bethel Seminary through their distance learning program. All of the preachers on staff utilized visuals in multiple and creative ways. We experimented with props, drama, video, and images. Our craft of visual preaching evolved with ever-expanding developments in technology.

Though I started with overhead projectors, it turned out that I was the only one interested in those. They seemed a little too "classroom-y" for the other preachers. The real technology was the 35mm slide projector. Yes, the results were snazzier, but the production process was more involved. If we wanted to project an image on a screen on Sunday morning, we had to submit our slides to the communications person by Wednesday. She had to run them to the photo developers' shop (remember those?), get them developed, and bring them back to church in time for us to proof them and make sure they would be OK. If they weren't right, she had to run them back to the developers and pay for a rush job. There were many nail-biting moments for preachers wondering if their slides would make it into the projector carousel in time for the service on Sunday morning.

The biggest, most life-changing moment for us as visual preachers in the 1990s was the invention of PowerPoint and the video projector. Suddenly the shackles of film development fell from our feet, and we were able to run free in the open fields of color, animation, and last-minute edits! It was glorious.

This was the ideal environment for me to grow as a visual preacher. We were an evangelical megachurch. We had fought the worship wars and fully embraced the weekend service as a Willow Creek–style, "seeker-targeted" event. We were willing to use any media available to create a culturally relevant message that would pave the way and "open hearts" to receive the gospel.

This spirit of openness and innovation allowed us to embrace new technology as it emerged on the market. There were no "sacred spaces" that would seem defiled by screens and drum sets and theatrical lighting.

We evolved and by the early 2000s had moved into a massive, three-thousand-seat facility with state-of-the-art technology. We had a rock band that matched anything on the Las Vegas Strip. We had Jumbotron projectors, smoke machines, gobo lights, video, live drama.

And I was tired.

Visual Preaching in Mainline Churches

The chances are that you, dear reader, are horrified by the last few paragraphs. This book is part of the Working Preacher Books series published by Fortress Press. The intended audience is preachers in the mainline denominations. You may preach in a gorgeous sanctuary with a pipe organ, beautiful vestments, and a congregation that loves high-church liturgy and classical music. You may be thinking, "Who let this evangelical preacher write a book for us? If that is visual preaching, then I'm out."

Let me go back to my previous statement: I was tired.

I am incredibly grateful for my experience at that church and all that I learned about visual preaching, large church dynamics, and leadership. But my theological imagination had expanded to the point that I could no longer authentically function within that context.

The decision to leave a megachurch meant leaving a steady paycheck. I remember driving across town after turning in my resignation and having a conversation with God: "OK, Lord, now what? I only know two ways to make a living. Either I'm a vocational pastor or I draw funny pictures." So I decided to open a freelance illustration and animation studio.

I spent the next five years quietly planting a network of house churches while I made a living as an artist. Suddenly I had no pulpit. There was no preaching. The house church community agreed to read through the Bible together throughout the week. We gathered in homes on Sunday mornings to pray, worship, share what God had taught us through our daily readings, and eat together on a day of Sabbath rest.

It was beautiful.

What does this have to do with visual preaching? A rhythm emerged during those five years. Each week I would study the text one week ahead of the church. Then I would do two things. First, I would draw a cartoon image that attempted to visually summarize the readings. Second, I would write a short "Food for Thought" commentary on each reading. I created a PDF document with the full-color cartoon illustration and the daily commentaries and emailed it to every member of the church. They had the option to use this as a study guide to help them work through the readings. I also posted the illustrations and notes on our website for anyone to access and share. (Remember, I had an art studio, so all of this technology was built into my daily rhythm of life.)

This is how "A Cartoonist's Guide to the Bible" was born. It wasn't called that back then. It was simply a section of my website called the "Bible Bookshelf." It was not traditional preaching, but it was visual communication intended to proclaim the gospel and engage people in Scripture. I spent hundreds, maybe even thousands of hours during those five years learning how to use digital media tools like Adobe Photoshop, Illustrator, Dreamweaver for web design, Adobe Flash for animation, Corel Painter, and Adobe Premiere Video Editor, to name a few.

The house church season of my life also allowed me time and space to grow theologically. I was immersed in the theological conversation known as the emerging church movement. I read Leonard Sweet, Stanley Grenz, Dallas Willard, Rachel Held Evans, Nadia Bolz-Weber, Spencer Burke, Richard Rohr, Brian McLaren, Michael Frost, Doug Pagitt, Tony Jones, and more.

I, like many young evangelicals, was on a trajectory that took me out of the ultraconservative turn evangelism was experiencing in the 2000s and into a more ecumenical wondering about the nature of God, the church, and how we are to be in the world. The journey has been difficult. In many ways I feel like how I imagine the explorers must have felt when they set sail from their homeland with no guarantee that there was a new shore on the other side of the ocean.

Sadly, our beautiful house church experience unraveled because many people were not in the same exploratory mindset I experienced. Things got ugly. The church died. I was crushed and went into a ministry coma for three years. We—my wife, four kids, and a dog—moved to Minnesota to be near my parents and hit the reboot button on life. I spent three years doing two things: (1) I tried to make a living as a freelance artist/animator, and (2) I used all my illustrations, daily commentaries, and web design knowledge to create a series of books and digital resources and took the Bible Bookshelf online.

God brought a Lutheran pastor across my path during those years. Pastor Mark befriended me, and we shared coffee meetings for a year. God used him to slowly melt my frozen heart and invite me back into ministry. I started off as a consultant for his church to help them work on adult spiritual formation. This was my first encounter with the Evangelical Lutheran Church in America (ELCA). It did not take long before I discovered that this church had a big tent and a theological air that allowed me to breathe again. The theology fed my soul, and the liturgical practices were a foreign language that has taken a while to learn and appreciate.

I transferred my ordination into the ELCA. I spent the next seven years learning the beauty of liturgy from this pastor while serving as his associate and earning a PhD in congregational mission and leadership from Luther Seminary. This combination was the perfect blend for me. Pastor Mark was helping this congregation live in the space between traditional liturgical worship in two services and a more informal, band-led worship style in the other two services. I was able to learn the beauty of liturgy on one hand while offering my experience in "contemporary" worship on the other. Pastor Mark had already laid the difficult groundwork of installing screens and video projectors in the sanctuary and opening up the congregation's mind to accept the presence of a drum set next to the chancel.

I was preaching again and immediately did what I do naturally: I incorporated cartoons, videos, and animation into my preaching. Here's the surprising thing. This Lutheran congregation loved it. They allowed me to be creative, experiment, and use all forms of visuals, including props, live painting on canvas, and drama, as well as projected images during sermons.

Why This Story Matters

That brings me to this moment in 2021, as I write these words. I have since taken a new call in an ELCA congregation that is larger and equally open to experimentation with visuals in preaching and various media. I met the people at Working Preacher through my work at Luther Seminary. They knew how much the use of visuals was a part of my life. It made sense to them to invite me to write this book for you.

I tell you this story for a few reasons.

First, you need to know how much I authentically use visuals in preaching. Some may argue that I do it too much. That is a fair assessment. Asking me to not use visuals, however, would be like asking me not to breathe.

Second, I want to assure you that you don't have to be like me to effectively use visuals in preaching. You don't have to be an artist. You don't have to be a technological wizard. You just need to be you. Take the things I offer to you in this book for what they're worth. They are my experiences. I will try to offer basic principles that I've learned along the way. Use the ones that make sense to you, and throw out the rest.

Third, I believe stories matter. Everything is a story, and all good storytelling utilizes imagery of some sort: metaphor, symbolism, luscious descriptive prose, and . . . visuals. Preachers are storytellers. This book is part of my story, and I share it with you in the hope that it may become part of your story and that it will help you create effective images that make you an even better storyteller than you already are.

PART ONE

Foundations for Visual Preaching

1

We Wish to See Jesus

Why Use Visuals in Preaching?

The stack of flat brown boxes arrived in my driveway. This was not what I was expecting when I ordered a gazebo for my backyard patio. The photos online showed a beautiful structure with four posts and a roof that would provide shade for my outdoor patio. The opened boxes revealed hundreds of seemingly unrelated parts. Some assembly was required. How was I going to move from a box of parts to the functional gazebo I desired?

I was thankful for the instruction manual. However, the print was small and there were so many words. I started reading and was quickly overwhelmed. How would I ever make sense of how these words connected to these parts?

Do you know what saved me? Pictures.

I am a visual learner, so when I saw clearly illustrated step-by-step instructions, it put my mind at ease. I could easily connect the drawing of the part to the actual part in the box and visualize how the parts fit together. The pictures spoke a thousand words and showed me how to assemble the gazebo.

Preaching is like that. The people who sit in our pews are trying to make sense out of their lives. It can often seem like life is a box full of unconnected, unrelated parts, piled in an intimidating stack in the driveway. They have been told that the Bible has something to say about how to put it all together, but when they open the Bible it's just a bunch of words.

So. Many. Words.

The preacher's job is to relate the words to their lives in a way that helps them know how to connect all the parts. The ELCA discovered in the early 2000s that the average church member was essentially biblically illiterate. There was a major disconnect between the words of the Bible and their everyday lives. The ELCA launched the Book of Faith initiative to help correct this problem. After the initial five-year campaign ended, researchers discovered that the initiative had failed to hit its mark. The main problem was that preachers were not connecting it to the congregations through their preaching. Dave Daubert, a Lutheran pastor and PhD in theological studies, says that when the preacher does their job, those same people will find Scripture as a place to start a conversation about God, a "source and norm" for the faith that gathers them each week. From that base they will encounter the God who has come among us in Christ. That encounter with Christ will help what started in the past to become a present reality. And if it goes well, people will discover or rediscover that Jesus loves them and that their lives matter. They will feel useful to God and be sent back to their lives to be a part of what God is up to in the world in which they live every day.[1]

Karoline Lewis, professor of biblical preaching at Luther Seminary, says that the purpose of preaching is to "embody the Word."[2]

Think about that for a moment. A word is an abstract concept. It can be spoken into the air and received by the vibrations of sound waves on the eardrum. The brain decodes these vibrations into a culturally accepted meaning. That is the spoken word. A word can also be written. Text on a page or screen is an abstract visual code that must be taught, received by the brain, decoded, and constructed into meaning. This is a complex process.

There is a fundamental disconnect between words and basic human understanding. We require a certain level of education for words to make sense. The more complex the words are, the more sophisticated the training required to decode and understand the words becomes. Even as I type these words, I realize that I am excluding many people from connecting to the thing that I am trying to communicate.

But if I draw it . . .

Think about your own experience just now. Compare your experiences of (a) reading the words of the last few paragraphs that talked about human communication and (b) viewing the illustration above. In what ways were they similar? In what ways were they different? Pictures speak differently from words.

What did Lewis mean when she said, "Word"? She may have meant any spoken word, for, indeed, preaching is a performative act of speaking words into the air so people can hear them. However, she could have also intended the theological meaning of the term. The first verse of the Gospel of John says, "In the beginning was the Word." The Greek term is *logos*. Brian McLaren—an author, speaker, activist, and public theologian—says that the Logos is like the blueprint (or the operating system) for the universe. The Logos is the abstract idea for existence itself. The finite human brain cannot begin to comprehend the vast complexity of the blueprint for everything.

The Word remains abstract and out of touch.

Until something amazing happens.

John's Gospel goes on to talk about the Word. In verse 1:14 it says, "The Word became flesh and lived among us." This verse is describing the person of Jesus. The abstract, creative power of God's blueprint for the universe took on a human body.

Jesus embodied the Word.

Now finite human beings have something to look at and understand. It does not require sophisticated education for a human being to see another human being and immediately connect. "Oh, look! That thing is like me. I get it!"

Do you remember the story of my gazebo and the illustrated instructions? Had those instructions been only text, without pictures, it would have been far more difficult to follow them, especially if the user cannot read English. It requires a certain amount of education, within a particular cultural language, to decode the written instructions to assemble the gazebo. Yet the drawings do not require the ability to read written language to understand. An illiterate person could look at the drawings, look at the pile of parts, and see how the parts fit together.

The purpose of preaching is to embody the Word. People need to see the Word in a way that makes sense to them and in a way that does not require a high amount of sophisticated education to decode.

The Hebrew Scripture is filled with stories of messengers who would proclaim the good news that the King was arriving, that "here is your God!" (Isa 40:9). The Hebrew term for this messenger of good news is *bsr*. It is translated in the Septuagint with the Greek term *euangelizomai*. This is the verb form of the term *euangelizo*. It literally means "good news." The English transliteration of the term is "evangelism."

Jesus's first sermon was simple and went like this, "The kingdom of God has come near; repent, and believe in the good news!" (Mark 1:15). The good news is that the kingdom of God is here. It is standing right in front of them. Jesus is the Logos in the flesh. Jesus is the drawing who showed them how the parts fit together. Watch Jesus live his life and you will see what it looks like to live in a covenant relationship with God and how to love God and love your neighbor.

Preaching is a performative act that is a physical embodiment of the gospel.

The problem we have is that we, in the twenty-first century, cannot see the physical body of Jesus like they did in the first century. The four Gospels and the writings of the first church provide our only opportunity to see Jesus. Ironically, the Bible itself has distorted our view of Jesus. The Word that was made flesh in Jesus has been translated back into words and made abstract and disconnected from us.

Good preaching embodies the Word so people can see it.

JOHN 1:1-4, 14
IN THE BEGINNING WAS THE
WORD
λόγος
AND THE WORD WAS WITH GOD
AND THE WORD WAS GOD
HE WAS WITH GOD IN THE BEGINNING
ALL THINGS CAME INTO BEING THROUGH HIM
AND WITHOUT HIM NOT ONE THING CAME INTO BEING
WHAT HAS COME INTO BEING
IN HIM WAS LIFE AND THE LIFE
WAS THE
OF ALL PEOPLE
AND THE WORD FLESH AND LIVED
BECAME AMONG US.
© 2017 STEVE THOMASON

When Mary Magdalene went to the garden tomb, she encountered the risen Christ. When she returned to the disciples she said, "I have seen the Lord" (John 20:18). She didn't describe Jesus with words or theology. She simply declared that she had seen him.

When the Greeks approached Philip in John 12:21, they announced, "Sir, we wish to see Jesus."

When Jesus began his ministry, the disciples asked him, "Where are you staying?" He did not respond with a verbal description of his house or verbal directions to get there. He said, "Come and see" (John 1:38–39).

This experience is what our congregations are asking for when they listen to our preaching.

"Preacher, we wish to see Jesus."[3]

People learn in many different ways. Pure words are very difficult for many people. Pictures and visual cues help connect the dots for a vast majority of the people in our pews. My goal for this book is to offer you practical ways to combine visual communication with the Word of Scripture and the words of your sermon, so that when you are done preaching, your listeners will say, "We have seen Jesus."

A Brief Theology of Visual Preaching

Even if the goal of our preaching is to enable our listeners to see Jesus, we—word-oriented as most preachers are—might still wonder, "Why should we use visuals in preaching?" Some preachers may be resistant to the use of visuals for various reasons. Some might think it is just a gimmick or an attempt to entertain people. Won't we run the risk of "dumbing down" the gospel?

Some preachers may be skeptical of using images because they realize that images are open to interpretation. Show an image to ten people with no verbal explanation and you will receive ten interpretations of what that image might mean. Some preachers are nervous that an image projected on a screen might illicit an interpretation that does not correlate with the intent of their sermon. Let's be honest. Preachers generally like to have control of what is spoken and how it is received.

These are legitimate concerns. Some preachers have succumbed to the idea that the church is competing with popular media. These preachers think they must be flashy and attuned to the type of media the congregation encounters every day in order to be relevant. These preachers might be so concerned with the special effects of the sermon that they forget the sermon itself.

It is also true that visual images without verbal explanation are open to interpretation. I would argue, however, that this openness is not a bad thing. A visual image opens the congregation to an interaction with the sermon that goes beyond words and engages much more of their brain. I am deeply convinced that human communication is, at its core, a visual act as well as a verbal one. I am also convinced that visual communication lies at the heart of the gospel itself.

The Case from Scripture

The Bible itself starts with the dynamic interplay of words and vision: "In the beginning when God created the heavens and the earth, the earth was a formless void and darkness covered the face of the deep, while a wind from God swept over the face of the waters. Then God said, 'Let there be light'; and there was light. And God saw that the light was good; and God separated the light from the darkness" (Gen 1:1–4).

Notice how things begin. Everything is a formless void. Darkness covers the face of the deep. Many scholars believe that "the deep" is another way of saying "chaos" or "disorder."

Then God speaks: "Let there be light."

Words emerge from the infinite creative force. Notice what the words do. They create some*thing* called light.

Notice what happens next. God *sees* that the light is good. Now that there is a something called light, and now that God can see it, God takes the first step toward bringing order out of the chaos.

God separates the light from the dark.

The story continues to reveal an ever-unfolding, increasingly complex spectrum of colorful forms and creatures.

And God sees these things because there is light.

And God calls it all good.

Notice what doesn't happen.

God doesn't speak words and allow them to hang in the abyss of darkness and chaos. God doesn't articulate an abstract argument about formlessness and darkness and chaos and three points to overcome them.

God speaks, and the words become a something.

God creates humanity and says that these creatures are the "image" and "likeness" of God. When you see these physical creatures, you see God.

The words take on a body.

The word becomes flesh, and God sees that it is very good.

Moses climbs to the top of Mt. Sinai and encounters the Divine. He receives many words that describe how the people can love God and love one another. The words of the covenant, found in Exodus 19–24, are abstract words. That is true. However, the words he receives in Exodus 25–31 are instructions on how to build a beautiful tent called the Tabernacle. This tent is a work of art, hand embroidered with intricate designs and filled with skillfully crafted furnishings.

Why a work of art?

The words of God's law and promise are not enough for the people. They need something tangible, something they can see. This visible display offers them a focal point so that the words of the covenant can take on a form that they can see, touch, and understand.

The Hebrew Bible is full of stories in which God directly communicates important truths and instructions to an individual. God almost never shows up as pure words. God shows up as a burning bush (Exod 3:1–4:17), a warrior (Josh 5:13–15), images of a severed heifer and floating pot (Gen 15), a dramatic creature with four heads on a flaming chariot (Ezek 1), a story of a vineyard (Isa 5:1–7) or a shepherd (Jer 3:15), a naked prophet cooking with his own feces (Ezek 4), and so forth.

The Word of God is almost always intertwined with a dynamic visual element.

Jesus was the master of visual communication. He didn't only tell his disciples that it was important to meditate on Scripture and learn to love their neighbors. He said, "I am the vine and you are the branches." He gave them an image that was very familiar to them and let them picture it in their mind's eye. He compared the kingdom of God to all sorts of everyday images: yeast, a seed, a pearl, a treasure. He told stories about shepherds and parents and fields. He told people they were shining lights and houses that should be built on rocks.

Jesus spent as much time showing his disciples how to live and love as he did telling his disciples about what it means to love God and our neighbors. The Bible is a grand narrative that shows us how God works in the world through living pictures of people's lives. We, too, as proclaimers of the good news, would do well to do more showing than telling. The use of good visuals is a good start.

A Case from Educational Research

There is a reason God communicates visually throughout Scripture, I believe. It is because visual communication is an important way in which humans learn. Research shows that communication that combines words with visuals dramatically increases learning comprehension and retention. Words are abstractions that speak only to the logical, rational center of the brain.

Please understand, I am not suggesting that we preach only with visuals. I am suggesting a multisensory approach to preaching that engages the whole person. Richard Jenson, a Lutheran pastor and theologian, reminds us, "Our words need images in order to appeal to the artistic imagination. Our images, on the other hand, need words to protect us from mere superstition and idolatry. We need a kind of stereo homiletics that plays on the channel of word and the channel of image. Such preaching seeks to reach the whole of the human person."[4]

A text-only method of communication is good, but it is limited in two ways. First, the human brain must be conditioned by much training in rational thinking and the processing of words in order to comprehend them. It takes a highly disciplined and specially trained mind to be able to focus and process words alone. The spoken word alone excludes those who have not been trained in this particular mode of education (what in Western tradition we might call "higher education"). Put simply, a sermon that consists of pure words of abstract theological propositions will not connect to the average listener. They just haven't been trained to think that way.

Such a sermon is limited in another way. Words alone speak to only one-third of the human intelligence system. Cynthia Bourgeault, an Episcopal priest and theologian, argues that humans have three centers of intelligence: the rational intelligence, the movement intelligence, and the emotional intelligence. We also know these centers as the mind, the body, and the spirit. The mind processes abstract information and observes nature through dissection and analysis. The body experiences the physical reality of the universe and knows by doing. The spirit encounters the universe and empathically connects through intuition or emotion.

Words speak more to the mind, especially if the words are purely didactic and not attempting to tell a story or paint a word picture.

Visuals, on the other hand, connect to the body and the spirit. We physically see an image or object. The image connects to the viewer in a way that moves beyond rational thought and relates the image to lived experiences, of both body and spirit, that the viewer may not be able to articulate or hear in words. When this visceral, suprarational experience of viewing the image is combined with compelling words that connect to Scripture, then preachers can more effectively help the congregation see the good news. We can help them see Jesus and how the gospel connects to their own lived experience.

The Limitations of Images

Images have limitations too. There are certain risks involved when using visual elements in a sermon. In fact, there are certain risks involved with all styles of preaching. The risk has to do with the limitations we all experience as humans.

I'm talking about *frames*.

A frame is a limit that is placed around something. We all have them, and they impact the way we understand the world around us and how we communicate with one another. It is important for the preacher to be aware of these frames.

There are three types of frames that might help us explore the limitations around the use of images and our ability to clearly communicate with one another. The first type of frame is the boundary within which a photographer or painter captures an image. A camera has a rectangular window that only reveals a small portion of the environment. The photographer must choose what to place inside the frame and what to leave out. A painter has limited space on the canvas and must create a composition within its boundaries. Discerning viewers recognize that what is outside the frame is as important as what is captured in the frame and are curious about what they cannot see. When a preacher chooses an image, it is important to keep this concept of framing in mind. Who is in the picture? Who is not in the picture? What might the inclusion or exclusion of elements in this image communicate?

The second type of frame is structural. Carpenters frame a house with wood. They build the basic structure that determines the shape and stability of everything else that will follow in the construction process. Computers also have a framework. The configuration of the hardware and the software operating system determines how the applications will function. Humans have a similar structural framework. This framework is often called a worldview or a presupposition. It is the lens through which we perceive reality. Most often we are not aware that we have a lens and thus assume that the way we perceive reality is reality itself. Every person that comes into your sanctuary to hear your sermon brings with them a frame like this. They have a perspective that is based on their life experience. They will only experience your sermon through their own framework, not yours.

It is impossible to completely understand everyone else's framework, nor is it possible to speak to every framework within one sermon. Yet it is important for the preacher to be aware of multiple perspectives and be as considerate and cognizant of them as possible within any sermon. At the very least, the preacher can acknowledge that they are preaching from within a framework that shapes the message itself and give permission for the audience to receive it within their own framework.

The third type of frame has to do with time. Think of how movies work. Motion pictures travel at a rate of twenty-four frames per second (thirty per second for video). Movies are sequences of still images that create the illusion of movement when run together at high speed. A single frame from a motion picture is a static snapshot—frozen in time—that tells only a fraction of the larger story. It is accurate but incomplete.

A sermon is a single frame. It is a performative act where a preacher presents a sermon to a particular group of people in a particular moment in time. The sermon attempts to connect the dots between the historical document of Scripture, the current events important to that particular audience, the individual lives within the congregation, and what God might be doing in the midst of it today. People and circumstances change over time. Preachers evolve theologically. Churches have new lived experiences that change the composition of the congregation. Things change constantly. A sermon that worked really well today might not have the same meaning or impact in a year. A visual image that makes sense today might seem outdated or even offensive in five years. The preacher must always keep the framework of time in mind when choosing both words and images for a sermon.

I began this section talking about the risks involved in communicating. The limitations of the frames listed above do create challenges for preaching. However, the risk is worth taking. Everything worth doing involves risk. Multisensory communication is complicated, but it is vital. Preachers must be aware of the limitations, prayerfully consider the words and images for a sermon, trust in God's presence to work in and through the sermon, then boldly proclaim the good news, limitations and all.

2

You Don't Have to Be an Artist

Studying the Bible Visually

Visual preaching begins at the same place all preaching begins—with the preacher and the biblical text. In this chapter, I will offer you some basic principles for how to study the biblical text visually and identify or create an image that will quickly summarize the central idea of the text. Don't worry, you don't have to know how to draw. Throughout this book, keep these two principles in mind:

1. You *do not* have to be an artist to be a visual preacher.
2. You can be a visual preacher *without using digital technology.*

If you can make lines and basic shapes, then you will be able to visually study the text.

Breaking Down the Block

When we first open the Bible, we are confronted with a massive block of text. It can be overwhelming. The first question that a preacher must ask of a text is, "What is the central idea of the text itself? What does it say?"

The first step to uncovering the text's meaning is to break it down. One way to do that is to create a simple outline.

Let me show you what I mean by visually analyzing Ephesians 3:14–19.

1. Begin with the Block of Text

You can read directly from your Bible, or you can type the text out and print it on a clean piece of paper. If you have a Bible software program, you can copy and paste the text from there, or go to an online Bible (such as Biblia.com, BibleGateway.com, or BibleHub.com) and copy and paste from there.

Take a moment to prepare yourself to encounter the text. Take a deep breath. Ask God to slow down your mind and open your eyes and heart to see the text in a new way.

Read the text a few times. Perhaps read it out loud.

[14] For this reason I bow my knees before the Father, [15] from whom every family in heaven and on earth takes its name. [16] I pray that, according to the riches of his glory, he may grant that you may be strengthened in your inner being with power through his Spirit, [17] and that Christ may dwell in your hearts through faith, as you are being rooted and grounded in love. [18] I pray that you may have the power to comprehend, with all the saints, what is the breadth and length and height and depth, [19] and to know the love of Christ that surpasses knowledge, so that you may be filled with all the fullness of God.

2. Mark Your Text

Now grab a pencil, and perhaps a highlighter or some colored pencils.

Start noticing things. Are there key phrases that raise questions in your mind? Are there repeated words or phrases? Is there a logical pattern of thought? Are there obvious metaphors, similes, or word pictures?

> "I am suffering so that the GENTILES can know the Mystery of God's love"

> this seems like MORE than PRAYER. This is submission to Authority.

¹⁴(For this reason) I bow my knees before the Father, ¹⁵ from whom every family in heaven and on earth takes its name. ¹⁶ I pray that, according to the riches of his glory, he may grant that you may be strengthened in your inner being (with power through (his Spirit) ¹⁷ <and> that Christ may dwell in your hearts through faith, as you are being rooted and grounded in love. ¹⁸ I pray that you may have the power to comprehend, with all the saints, what is the breadth and length and height and depth, ¹⁹ <and> to know the love of Christ that surpasses knowledge, [so that] you may be filled with all the fullness of God.

Allow me to explain my initial markings.

The phrase "for this reason" begs the reader to go back and read what has come before the text. The "reason" will provide context for our paragraph.

One point is repeated: "I bow my knees" (v. 14), "I pray" (v. 16), and "I pray" (v. 18). It seems like this is Paul's prayer for the people.

The key word "and" marks three distinct things for which Paul is praying. Notice that I highlight these connectors in < > brackets and write the numbers 1, 2, and 3 directly in the text.

3. Make an Outline

Now take a blank piece of paper.

Create an outline. Pay close attention to prepositional phrases. They usually modify the thing just before them and thus need to be indented.

Here is how I arranged this text in an outline.

FOR THIS REASON,
    I bow my knees
      before the Father
        from whom every family
          in heaven and on earth
          takes its name.
I PRAY THAT,
    according to the riches of his glory,
he may grant that you:
① MAY BE STRENGTHENED
    in your inner being
      with POWER
      through HIS SPIRIT.
AND ② that CHRIST may DWELL
    in your HEARTS
    through FAITH
    AS you are being
      ROOTED + GROUNDED
      in LOVE
I PRAY
③ that you may have the POWER to COMPREHEND
    with all the saints
What is the
  BREADTH +   AND TO KNOW
  LENGTH +   THE LOVE of CHRIST
  HEIGHT +   that surpasses
  DEPTH,   Knowledge
SO THAT
you may be FILLED
  with ALL the FULLNESS of GOD.

Notice how this outline allows the eye to move through the passage in a different manner. The three main requests of Paul's prayer become obvious. Paul prays

1. that you may be strengthened,
2. that Christ may dwell in your hearts, and
3. that you may have the power to comprehend.

Notice the two key words in the paragraph: "so that." Why does Paul pray these things for the people? He prays "so that" they may be filled with all the fullness of God.

When we outline the text like this, it allows us to see the many layers from which we can glean great preaching material.

For example, in petition 1, Paul prays that you may be strengthened. OK. What does that mean? How? Is this about physical power?

The outline creates more white space in the text and allows us to see the logical flow. We can begin to have a conversation with the text:

- What kind of strength? In your inner being.
- What does it look like? It looks like power. But what is power? Let me look up the Greek word. It is *dunamis*. I study the Greek word and realize that *dunamis* means "energy" and "ability to do something."
- How do we get this kind of power? It comes through God's Spirit. It is not from ourselves but by God's Spirit, giving us the inner ability to accomplish things.

This process, and the insights it brings forth, might be all you need to begin crafting your sermon. However, let me show you another way to visualize the text. This process may open new pathways of thought for the sermon.

Make a Visual Map

Use arrows, boxes, and basic symbols to arrange the words in a map that communicates the meaning of the text in a different way.

Here is a map I created from our Ephesians text. Notice what I did.

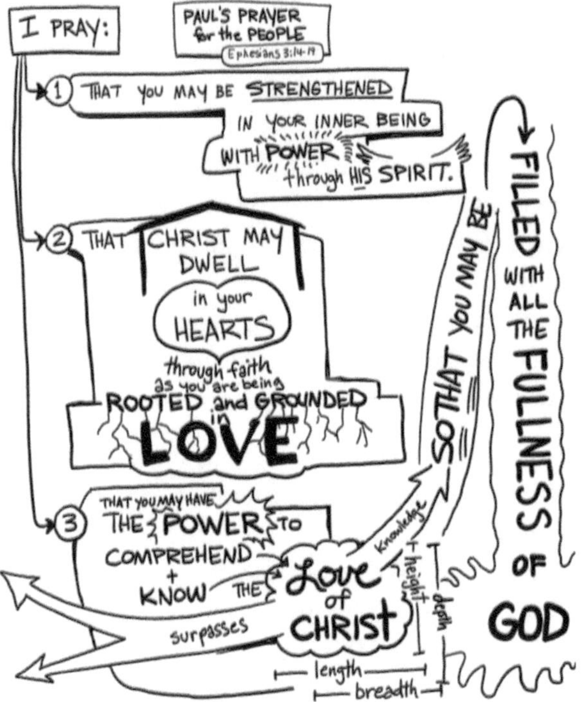

First, I gave it a title, "Paul's Prayer for the People," and highlighted the main action, "I pray," in a box.

Second, I enclosed each of the three petitions in a box.

Third, I created a mini mind map within each petition to visually represent what the words communicate.

Notice that I'm still using the basic outline structure but adding underlines and marks around words. Energy lines radiate from "power," and the word "spirit" has wings, like the dove.

I place a simple house frame around the words "Christ may dwell" and the heart symbol around "in your hearts." It's obvious, but the icons help draw out the meaning.

Notice the placement of the words "rooted and grounded." They are above the word "love" and roots grow from them into the word.

There is a lot going on in the third petition. Paul prays that the Ephesians may have power (ability) to *comprehend* and *know*. The prayer is not for general comprehension and knowledge of all things. It is specifically that they would comprehend and know the love of Christ. Therefore, I emphasized the words "love of Christ" in the cloud and drew arrows from "comprehend" and "know" to the cloud. It is obvious what the focus is supposed to be.

Paul also uses several words and phrases to describe the love of Christ. It surpasses knowledge and it is beyond measure in height, depth, length, and breadth. I place these words in a way that visually illustrates their meaning. "Surpasses" and "knowledge" move beyond the boundaries of the box. The four measurement words are marked like dimensions on a blueprint, measuring the cloud.

Finally, I take the "so that" and try to depict the act of filling by flowing the words down the side of the page.

Notice how many words it took for me to describe what I did in the drawing. Yet you probably got all that, and a lot more, by simply looking at it.

That's the power of visual communication.

Imagine what would happen if you simply walked your congregation through that process and called it a sermon. As you display each section of this illustration on the screen and talk through the text, your congregation will be able to see what you mean as you speak and build a visual, multisensory memory of the text that will help them remember it far longer than if you simply read it to them. As they see the symbols you choose to illustrate the outline, they might think of how they might have chosen to illustrate it, thus helping them make more connections.

Putting It All Together

You've broken down the text by outlining it, making marks all over it, and drawing pictures in and beside it. It probably looks like a mess: a beautiful mess. There is a final step that might help create a nice springboard to launch into the construction of the sermon itself. Remember, all we've been concerned with until this point has been to understand the text itself and what it says. We'll worry about how to present it clearly in a sermon in the next chapter.

The final step is to create a visual chart that summarizes all your discoveries in the text. Take a step back from your beautiful mess. Do you observe patterns in the text? Do you see key themes? How might you create a visual chart that quickly summarizes your findings?

You may build upon the visual outline from the previous section. Get a clean piece of paper, or a new page on your screen, and clean it up. Write the main points in large letters. Draw key symbols in a pattern that easily communicates the organizational structure of the text and the central idea.

Here is what I've done with the Ephesians text.

Notice how this process took us from a solid block of text to this dynamic visual tool.

You might end up using this graphic in your sermon, or you might not. Either way, you have a strong visualization of the text that will create a framework upon which you can construct a sermon.

3

Maps and Boxes

Visually Constructing a Sermon

Once you have visually analyzed the text itself, it is time to start creating a sermon that connects the central idea of the text to your congregation and the issues that matter to them in their everyday lives. We can use several techniques to visually brainstorm ideas for the sermon and organize them into a final presentation. All of these ideas can be accomplished either with paper and pencil or digitally.

Brainstorming the Sermon

I will offer two methods to visually brainstorm. The first is by drawing on one piece of paper. This is called *mind mapping*. The second is by using separate pieces of paper and arranging and rearranging them in different configurations. This is called *creative storyboarding*. The principles are the same for both media.

Mind Mapping

A mind map is an organic, nonlinear way to brainstorm ideas and later see how they are connected. Here is a simple description of the process.

First, begin with a central idea. A sermon usually begins with one of two things: a specific *text* or a specific *topic*. Write the text or topic in the center of a piece of paper. This might not be the central idea by the time you finish thinking through your sermon. It might end up being a subpoint of the sermon. You might abandon it altogether in the end. It doesn't matter. The point is that you start with something and start branching out from it.

Second, begin writing ideas about this central idea near it and around it. You might arrange the ideas in the first ring of a set of concentric circles or radiating from the central idea. I find creating branches from a central trunk to be a helpful process.

As I begin capturing the ideas a text inspires, I often write one idea and branch out from it into further subideas, then move on to the next big idea. There is no correct order or pattern in which the ideas must emerge. You can draw a new branch as it naturally emerges. Eventually, you will have a mind map like this.

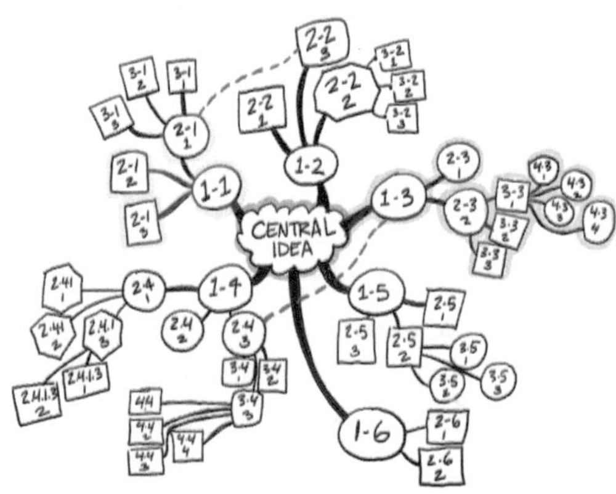

Spend some time meditating on this beautiful mess that you have created. Notice if any patterns emerge. You may realize that you completely missed a level-one (first-ring) idea. That's OK. Just add it.

Meditate on the map a little more. Ask God to reveal patterns to you. You may want to use markers or colored pencils to start highlighting patterns and connections that emerge.

Here is an example of a topical mind map that I made when preaching on the question "How can we listen to God?"

Notice that I first placed the central idea in the middle of the paper: "Listening to God."

Whenever I preach on a topic, I first ask, "What does the Bible have to say about this?" So I drew a simple Bible icon as the first branch.

I did some Bible study and found three key texts that spoke to my question. Notice how they branch out from the Bible icon.

I tried to imagine the types of questions people might ask if we were having this discussion over coffee. "How does God speak?" "How can we discern that it is God's voice in a sea of noise?" "There are so many voices; how do we know which one is God's?"

The mind map at this point helps determine areas of focused study. You may or may not use each of these areas in your final sermon, but the exercise is a rich experience in itself.

Creative Storyboarding

The art of storyboarding was first developed by Walt Disney Studios in the 1930s as a way to talk through the sequence of an animated film. A storyboard is a series of images and words placed in a linear sequence to help visually organize a presentation or film. The idea is to quickly and roughly sketch out the various shots of a scene on small pieces of paper, usually index cards, and pin them to a wall. Each drawing shows only any significant change necessary to propel the story. These changes depict either a shift in the camera angle or an important movement of the character that impacts the story.

The storyboard artist's job is to pin up enough small sketches, in a series of rows reading left to right, to be able to talk through the scene with the rest of the animation team so that they understand the flow of the story.

A sermon is much like a movie or a stage play. It is a public performance of oratory art. It is also inherently visual, since the congregation is looking at the preacher and all the elements in which the preacher stands: the pulpit, the chancel or stage, the items on the stage, the decorations on the walls, and possibly a screen upon which digital images appear. All of these visuals will

capture the audience's attention and either work with or fight against the words that the preacher speaks. Storyboarding will help the preacher think through all of these elements before the sermon is delivered.

There are two phases to storyboarding: *creative storyboarding*, another form of brainstorming, and the *final storyboard*, which we will discuss in the next section.

Making Little Boxes

A storyboard is simply a series of little boxes. We have many tools at our disposal to create these little boxes. Some are simple, analog solutions. Some are digital.

The most basic form of storyboard is small pieces of paper. You may cut up plain printer paper into equal size rectangles.

The standard 3″ × 5″ index card is hard to beat. You may want to use the kind that has lines on one side and is blank on the other side. Sometimes you might want to write words on the lines. Sometimes you might want to draw a simple image on the blank side.

You might also use purchased sticky notes, the technological upgrade from the index-card-and-thumbtack method. The beauty of these is that they are small, come prestacked in easy-to-peel piles of squares, and can be placed on nearly any surface except those with texture or too much dust.

I would not recommend using a square any smaller than two or two and a half inches.

Write one idea per card or note and stick them to the wall. If you use paper of various colors, you can color code themes, topics, or types of material. For example:

- biblical references: blue
- illustrations: pink
- main ideas: yellow

As ideas flow to your mind, choose the appropriate color, write them on the paper, then stick it to the wall. The color blast that will emerge on your wall may start to display its own patterns if, in fact, the colors have predetermined categories.

Digital Boxes

Many digital tools can make the storyboarding process easy, fun, and transferrable to a final digital presentation. The most readily available tool is presentation software, such as PowerPoint, Keynote, or Google Slides. These software programs are essentially storyboarding tools—a sequence of boxes where you can capture ideas in text and images.

If you are going to end up using one of these tools to present your sermon, I suggest you begin with it in the brainstorming phase.

"I don't have digital projection in my preaching space," you may be thinking. "Should I skip this part?"

Perhaps. However, my guess is that even if you don't use projection in your preaching, you probably have a computer that has the ability to run one of these presentation programs (Google Slides is free, by the way). You could use the program to storyboard your sermon, then print it as a visual manuscript.

Here's how you can use these programs to make a storyboard:

- Think of each new slide as an index card or sticky note.
- Create a new slide for each individual idea. Type your idea or use the various drawing tools in the software to create a simple scheme. You don't have to be fancy.
- Keep making slides until you have exhausted your brainstorming process.
- Click on the thumbnail view. Now you have your wall of index cards or sticky notes. You can increase or decrease the size of the thumbnails to fit them all in the window.
- Then click and drag the slides to reorder them. The program automatically arranges the slides and renumbers them as you move the slides around.

This process is essentially no different from using pen and paper or sticky notes.

Drawing on a Computer

There is one potential drawback (pun intended) to using the computer, as opposed to pen and paper, to draw quick shapes or diagrams on the storyboard squares: it is difficult to draw on a computer using a mouse. In fact, I can say this as an artist: it is pretty much impossible to draw with a mouse.

There are two ways around this.

The first method is draw and import:

1. Draw your image on a piece of paper.
2. Snap a picture of the image with your phone and send the image to your computer.
   a. If you use a Mac, you can simply Airdrop the image to your desktop.
   b. If you are on a PC, you can email, text, or use whatever transfer method is native to your computer to get the image from your phone to the desktop.
3. Click "Insert" in the presentation software and place the image on your slide.

The second method is easier but requires an iPad or tablet with a stylus. With these tools, you can draw directly in the presentation software. Using a tablet makes the digital experience almost identical to the pen-and-paper experience.

What Do I Put in the Boxes?

Once you decide which technical process you will use to create the boxes for storyboarding, you need to think about what you actually write or draw in the boxes.

You don't have to be an artist to create a storyboard. Some of the best storyboards are comprised of words, stick figures, and shapes. Remember, too, that no one has to see your storyboard unless you choose to use it later in the actual presentation. For now, it is a tool to help you organize your thoughts and the elements of your sermon.

The beauty of creative storyboarding is that it begins in a nonlinear fashion. The key to success in the storyboarding process is to write or draw one idea in a box as the ideas come to your mind.

- What is the main text? Write each reference in a box.
- What are some key observations you've made about the text? Write each one in a separate box.
- Do you have any stories or humorous illustrations that might pertain to the text? Write each one in a separate box.
- Do you have any important quotes from Bible scholars or famous figures? Write each one in a separate box.

Keep creating new boxes in a flurry of creativity until you run out of steam. Now you have a pile of boxes with ideas in them.

The next step is to lay the squares out on a table, tape them to a wall, pin them to a corkboard, or view them on your screen.

Step back from the squares and begin to observe your beautiful mess. Move them around until they begin to take on a logical flow.

Remove boxes that no longer make sense in the flow. Add new ones as new ideas form. Mix them up. Form new patterns. Work until a pattern emerges that seems to make sense.

Now you are ready for the final step.

Final Storyboards

The beauty of brainstorming is that it is nonlinear and organic. The order in which you proceed through the process doesn't matter. You can follow as many wild rabbits as you want down trails that lead to wonderful discoveries, or to nowhere.

Eventually, however, the preacher is faced with the reality of the sermon itself and the context in which it will be delivered. As soon as the preacher stands in front of the congregation, the clock starts ticking, and time always proceeds in a linear manner. Each word, each idea, and each visual element must proceed in a linear sequence, one after another.

There are two ways to use the final storyboard. The first is to use it to visualize the physical space in which the sermon will be delivered. How will the preacher use the space? What objects in that space might add to or detract from the sermon? This is similar to how a stage director and/or set designer would storyboard a live performance. You might be thinking, "Um . . . I just stand in the pulpit and talk. How could this be helpful?" If you simply stand in the pulpit and never move your body during your sermon, then this type of storyboarding would not be helpful at all. However, if you are the type of preacher who likes to physically move around in the worship space during the sermon, then it might be helpful to visually storyboard where you might stand and what you might hold in your hand during each part of the sermon. We'll talk more about this style of preaching in part 2.

The second way to use the storyboard is to visually organize the flow of the sermon itself and the images that might be projected on a screen. Think of this as a visual outline. How will each point and visual element flow together as they are presented in a linear sequence? This is similar to how a filmmaker would storyboard the images that will appear in sequence during a film that is projected on a flat screen.

The process of creating the final storyboard is quite simple. Choose one little box from your brainstorming mind map or storyboard and place it on a line that moves from left to right. Place one box at a time, reordering the boxes as seems appropriate, until they are all in a row. The final storyboard helps organize the sermon in a linear fashion that reads like a visual manuscript. The storyboard can then be used to write a full manuscript for your sermon, if that is your style. Or you could use the storyboard as the manuscript that you take to the pulpit.

If you want to preach with more than key words or images at hand, you can write the words of your sermon next to each little box. Printable storyboard templates are available online that have a blank box with a block of blank lines next to it. You might use this to draw and write your sermon. Presentation software like PowerPoint usually has a notes section for each slide. Write the text of your sermon in the notes section and it will stay associated with that little box. Print the presentation in notes mode and you have a printed visual manuscript.

A website called StoryboardThat.com allows the user to create fully illustrated storyboards without needing the ability to draw. It comes with an extensive library of panel designs, backgrounds, characters, and settings.

The website was designed for educators to engage students in interactive and creative learning, but it could be an incredibly powerful tool for the preacher who would like to make compelling storyboards that have high-quality illustrations for the final preaching event.

Ultimately, storyboarding is a simple process of making a sequence of squares that tell a story. Find the method that is most comfortable and efficient for you and will allow you to visually create a sermon manuscript.

Now you are ready to present a visual sermon.

PART TWO

The Visual Sermon

4

Everything Communicates

Three-Dimensional Space

All preaching is visual, assuming you are preaching to a congregation that has the gift of physical sight. The congregation can see you. They can see what you are wearing. They can see where you are standing. They can see the objects and decorations that adorn the room in which you are preaching.

In fact, most preaching throughout history has been primarily visual. Think of the mosaics of the Byzantine churches and the spectacular murals, sculptures, and stained glass windows of the European cathedrals. All of this art was created to visually tell the story of Scripture.

Why? Because through much of the church's history, most people were illiterate. The printed text meant nothing to them. Additionally, much of the worship service was spoken in Latin, and the people didn't speak that language. So the spoken word meant nothing to them. They came to church to see the pictures and experience the liturgical movements of worship.

Engaging the Senses

This book is specifically about the use of visuals in preaching. However, it is important to note that preaching, and the entire worship experience, is a multisensory event. Always keep in mind that the sermon is one movement in the grand symphony of the worship service. The message of the event begins as people arrive at the church building and ends as they drive or walk away. Every part of the experience communicates the message. The weather will impact their mood and receptivity. The architecture, landscaping, and decoration outside of the building will greet them and set a tone for what they might encounter on the inside. Think of a visitor to your church. What signs are posted on the doors? What message does the entrance convey to the surrounding community? The temperature of the entryway will set a tone. What do people see when they step into the building? What do they smell? What do they touch, taste, and hear? Who do they encounter?

All of these sensations happen before they enter the sanctuary and set them up for worship. Now they sit and look to the front of the worship space. What do they see, hear, smell, feel before the service even begins? Are there colors in the chancel that evoke a mood or indicate a liturgical season? Do objects or images invite them to wonder about what might happen during the service? Does everything seem prepared in anticipation, or do they see people scurrying around in frantic, last-minute preparation or choir and band members chatting before the service like they are on a coffee break?

What Are the Visual Elements of Preaching?

There are many visual elements in a sermon. People see more than they hear. They see your body. They see the physical space in which you stand while preaching. They see the furniture and decorations of the room. They see the objects and images that you intentionally use as part of your sermon. A visual preacher must keep all these elements in mind while preaching.

Your Body

The first visual element of every sermon is you. People see you. They notice your clothes, your body, how you hold your body, where you are standing, whether you are fidgeting or confident. They notice your face and what mood it projects. Are you smiling or frowning? Are you focused on your notes or are you engaging the congregation? There are many nonverbal cues that communicate a tone for your sermon before you ever open your mouth.

It is important to keep two realities in tension when considering the fact that your physical body is the first visual element of a sermon. First, it should help you carefully consider what message your choice of clothing might convey to the congregation. This topic is highly contextual, and there is no ironclad right or wrong answer. Some contexts require clerical clothing—albs, stoles, and so on—for the preacher. In other contexts the same clothing could be off-putting and shut down the message before it begins. Know your audience, and be aware of how your physical appearance may communicate a particular message to your audience.

The second reality to keep in mind is that the preacher is a window to God. Our goal in preaching is not to have people leave the service saying, "Wow! Didn't Pastor do a great job today?" Instead, we hope that our preaching will cause people to forget that we are there and to have an authentic encounter with the Word of God that will touch their lives. We want them to see Jesus, not us.

This is a tricky tension. They can't help but see us. So it is important to make sure that how we present our bodies does not distract from the message but enhances it to communicate clearly and lead people to the risen Christ.

The Physical Space
Church architecture and the symbolic meaning of the physical worship space is a topic worthy of its own volume. It is important to note, for our purposes, that the physical space in which you preach has a visual and theological impact on the congregation before you utter a word. A sanctuary modeled after medieval European cathedrals intentionally carries theological meaning in every part of the room: the font is placed at the entrance so worshippers walk through their baptism to enter, the ceilings are lofted to draw our attention to God's transcendence, and so on. A worship service held in a rented school gymnasium might communicate the pragmatic nature of the congregation or the mobility of the church. A worship service that gathers around a campfire emphasizes the relational nature of God and the church as worshippers sit around a circle with a fire in the center. A visual preacher must be aware of the physical space and what it might intrinsically communicate.

Once the nature of the physical space itself is ascertained, it is also important for you to think about how to use the space when you preach. Where do you stand? Do you move around? Do the pieces of furniture in the room have symbolic meaning?

Do you stand in certain places during different parts of the sermon to make a particular point?

Let's talk honestly about pulpits. How do you feel and what do you think about them? They can be controversial. Some churches have a strong tradition that a preacher must always stand in the pulpit to preach. Some churches even distinguish between the lectern and the pulpit. The lectern is for the laypeople, and the pulpit is a sacred space where only clergy can proclaim the Word of God.

It is important to note that the pulpit has, in many traditions, conveyed the importance of God's Word. Much like the witness box in a courtroom, the pulpit is the physical space in which the vital testimony of God's Word is proclaimed.

It is also important to note that pulpits, as well as witness stands in the courtroom, were invented for a very practical reason: sound amplification. Before the invention of the loudspeaker and microphones, it was difficult to speak to a large audience and be heard. For centuries, churches and cathedrals were built with domes and arches to help sound travel. Pulpits were erected above the congregation, so the voice of the preacher could project to the back of the room. Public speaking needed to be bold and loud, simply so people could hear.

Do we need pulpits anymore?

Today with sophisticated sound systems, a small child can sit in a corner of the room and whisper, and every person in the room can feel intimately connected to her. Wireless microphones free the speaker from one location and offer the ability to move freely anywhere in the room. The preacher can even go outside the room and be heard. Multiple people can wear microphones and have a casual conversation and be heard clearly.

If your worship space has wireless microphone technology, then why not use the space fully? Perhaps you can stand in the pulpit when you read the text. Then move to the altar when talking about Jesus. Stand by the font when talking about the Holy Spirit. Stand in the middle of the congregation when talking about life application. The point is to explore ways that you can physically move your body to different parts of the room to emphasize different parts of your sermon.

Objects

We have seen how the preacher's body is a visual element and how that body stands in a physical space full of visual elements. Now let us focus on the act of preaching itself and the use of physical, visual elements. The most basic of these elements that can be introduced into a sermon is an object. Imagine you are going to preach on Jeremiah and the image of the potter. What if you had a potter's wheel sitting in the center of the chancel for the whole service? Or placed one in the narthex, so people walk past it as they enter? Or placed two or three clay pots on small tables in various places in the front of the worship space? The simple presence of these objects would pique the congregation's interest. Why are those objects sitting there? They aren't usually there, so what is going to happen in the service that is different? The object itself ignites a conversation with the congregation before the service begins. They will be eager for you to step up to preach so they can answer these questions.

Some Examples

Allow me to share some examples from my own preaching experience to demonstrate the use of physical space as visual preaching. Note that I am about to show you, rather than tell you, how to do this. I offer these journal entries as personal reflections that I wrote immediately following actual experiences of preaching in my own context.

People as Visual Aids

I did something in my sermon tonight that is a good example of how to use people in the congregation as a visual aid. The text was Mark 1:15. Jesus proclaimed, "The time is fulfilled, and the kingdom of God has come near; repent, and believe the good news." I told the congregation that the word "repent" is an English translation of the Greek word *metanoia*. This word means "to change one's mind" or "to change how you perceive reality." I found a wonderful explanation online while I was studying for the sermon that painted a picture of metanoia.

Imagine you are standing in a circle of people.

In the center of the circle, there is a source of light.

But rather than facing the center and the light, you are standing with your back to the light, facing outward.

When you stand this way, facing away from the light, all you can see is your own shadow.

You cannot see the light.

You can only look into your shadow.

You cannot see the others in the circle with you.

From what you can see, you are disconnected and alone in the dark.

Now imagine that you turn around to face the light that is in the center of the circle.

When you turn toward the light, you no longer see only darkness.

When you turn toward the light, your shadow is behind you.

When you turn toward the light, you can now see the other people who are standing with you.

You can see that the light is shining on everyone and that you are all connected in its radiance.

Making the decision to turn around, to turn away from shadow, to face the light: this is metanoia.[1]

I could have simply read that text to the congregation and allowed them to visualize it in their own imagination. But I had a different idea. I decided to follow the advice "Show, don't tell."

I invited four people to join me on the platform. While they came forward, I took a small table, set it in the middle of the platform, then placed a candle from the altar on the table.

"Please circle around this table with me," I said, "and imagine that this candle is a large, bright, warm campfire. It is dark outside, and we are out in the woods. Can you see it?"

I helped them form the circle. There were five of us standing around the flame.

"Now turn away from the fire."

I turned my body and faced outward and looked over my shoulder to make sure they were all doing the same. I then broke away from the circle and started asking questions.

"What do you see?"

One man said, "Flowers; it's very nice."

He was looking at the poinsettias that were sitting on the chancel from the Christmas Eve services.

"It's dark out, remember. We're outside."

Everyone laughed.

"Imagine it. What do you see?" I pressed him further. He struggled to imagine anything, but some of the others in the circle offered, "My shadow."

"That's right!" I replied. "Now who do you see?" I asked the group.

"No one," they said, after a moment of contemplation.

"That's right. When you are turned away from the fire, all you can see is your own shadow, and it seems like you are alone."

I joined them in the circle once again and faced outward.

"Now turn toward the fire."

We all turned and faced the flame.

"What do you see?" I asked them.

"The fire," one said.

"Yes!" I exclaimed. "When we face the fire, we see and feel its warmth. Where is our shadow?" I asked.

"It's behind us," the young woman replied, her face beaming.

"One final question," I continued. "Who do you see?"

"Each other," they all said, almost in unison.

"Isn't this beautiful?" I asked. "When we face the fire, we see one another. We see that we are connected by its light and warmth, and we are not alone."

I turned to face away from the flame again.

"This," I said, then started to slowly pivot toward the flame as I said the next words, "is what metanoia looks like. To turn around and change the way you perceive your reality."

I paused for a moment and looked at each of them.

"What is the constant in this image?" I asked.

"The fire," the young woman replied.

"And what changed?" I encouraged her to continue.

"We did," she said. "We changed our relationship to the fire."

"Yes!"

I invited the congregation to thank them with applause as they returned to their seats.

Many people commented after the service that they really connected with that visual and it will stick with them for a long time.

Using Multimedia

The text for the sermon was Mark 4:1–34. Jesus tells the crowd about some seed that fell on four types of soil and how the seed developed within each soil. Then when in private with his close disciples, he explained the parable of the soils and gave them three more parables.

My sermon combined four forms of visual communication: a printed document, a physical object on the stage, still images on the screen, and a video.

Two visual elements greeted the congregation as they entered worship. The first things they saw were two TV tray tables sitting on the platform. A flowerpot sat on one table. A watering can sat on the other.

The second visual they encountered was a document called "Grow Guide," which was stuffed in the bulletin and handed to them upon entering the worship space. The Grow Guide is a one-page, double-sided document. On one side are small group questions, written by our adult ministries director. These questions are designed to guide individuals and groups deeper into the text through structured conversation during the upcoming week. The other side of the page displays a full-color illustration I created for the text. I lifted up the Grow Guide during announcements and told them to keep it out because we would use it during the sermon.[2]

Through these physical objects and their placement, the sermon has already begun, even before the service starts. People look at the tables and the objects and wonder what is happening. People who browse through the bulletin before the service notice the illustration and wonder where this will lead.

The sermon begins.

"This time last year I went on a grand adventure. I went to a place I had never gone before.

"I listened to all seven of the Harry Potter books on Audible. Every time I got in the car, the audiobook would come on and pick up where the story left off. Sometimes I would take the long way to where I was going just to finish a good part of the story. It was awesome.

"Now that I've read all seven books, I'm pretty sure that I'm an expert in magic."

The congregation laughs.

"Would you like to see a magic trick?"

A child in the front row shouts, "Yes!" Everyone chuckles.

I click the button on the remote control and bring up a slide that simply says "Magic Trick" over a blue-ink splotch.

I stand behind the two tables. A package of seeds sits next to the flowerpot.

"Here I have an ordinary packet of seeds."

I pour some in my hand. Small purple seeds sit in my palm. I walk to the front row and show them to a few people.

"They're tiny, right?" *The people nod in agreement.*

I'm back up on the platform, standing behind the table on the left. I've removed the watering can and set it on the ground.

"I'm going to place one of these tiny seeds right here in the middle of the table."

I place the seed. I slide to the right and stand behind the table and the flowerpot.

"This is an ordinary flowerpot."

I show the pot to the people in the front row.

"What's in it?"

"Dirt," *they respond.*

"Yes, ordinary potting soil."

I press my finger into the dirt.

"I'm going to make a little hole and drop one little seed into the soil."

I drop the seed, then pick up the watering can.

"Now I'll add a little bit of water."

I pour water into the pot.

I set the can down, then dramatically wave my hands over the flowerpot and tap on the edge.

"Bing!"

I look up and smile at the crowd.

"Nice trick!" *one man blurts out. Several people chuckle.*

I don't say anything right away but simply walk back to the podium at center stage.

"This week we continue our series through the Gospel of Mark . . ."

I purposefully detach abruptly from the magic trick and launch into a fairly typical sermon. This is where the slides come into play. I use my storyboarding method to keep myself on track and walk the congregation through the text, using the step-by-step slides of the graphic novel–style illustration that they also have printed and hold in their hand.

I read the text from the Bible in my hand while the images guide them through the text.

This is a challenging text, because there is so much in it and there are so many directions I could go with a sermon. I tell them near the beginning, "I don't know why you came to church today. I don't know what you need to hear from God today. I am going to simply read through the text and pause at different points to let you soak it in and listen. Then when we get through it, I'll tell you what I needed to hear from this text this week. Is it a deal?"

I read through Jesus's explanations of the four soils that he gave to his private audience. After the third soil, I pause and allow several seconds of silence for people to reflect on the hard path, the rocky soil, and the thorny soil.

There are two key phrases that I highlight during the sermon that I will come back to at the end. First, I point out that the word "secret" in the phrase "to you has been given the secret of the kingdom" is an unfortunate translation. The Greek term is *musterion*, from which we get the word "mystery." In our culture, a secret connotes an intentional hiding. A mystery, on the other hand, is something that is inherently difficult to understand.

The second phrase has to do with the hard path. When I read the parable in the first part of the text, I stop after Jesus says that some seed fell on the hard path and birds came and ate it. I say, "Do you know what you call seed on a hard path?" A pause.

"Bird food." People chuckled. I repeat this when I talk about Jesus explaining to his disciples that Satan steals the Word away. "What is seed on a hard path? Bird food."

I continue to read the rest of the passage, emphasizing that Jesus gave the next three parables only to his disciples, not the crowd.

Once I finish reading through the text, I pause once again.

"I don't know what you needed to hear from these parables. But I want to share what I needed to hear."

I click the remote, and the "Magic Trick" slide appears again.

"Do you want to see the magic trick?"

Many people verbally say, "Yes," and many more vigorously nod.

I step back over to the two tables and stand directly behind the table with the single seed. I lean over and point at the seed.

"Do you know what this seed is now?"

Several people call out, "Bird food!"

"Yes," *I smile with delight.* "It is just a seed and will never change. A seed on a hard table is bird food."

I slide over to the flowerpot and gaze expectantly into it. I look up at the crowd with a face of wonder.

"Do you know what this seed is now?"

I pause and scan the crowd.

"It's just a seed that looks exactly like that one on the table. I just planted this seed, people. There is no magic!

"And that is why I hate this parable."

I click the remote and bring up a slide that highlights the parable where Jesus says that the kingdom of God is like a farmer who sows seed. He plants it, and then the seed grows while the farmer just waits. Eventually the harvest comes.

I then tell a story about a particularly painful period in my life when I had to wait for three years when it seemed like the thing that God had promised was a lost cause.

I step back behind the flowerpot.

"You see, I want to be Harry Potter. I want to be able to wave my magic wand and POOF!"

I dramatically point at the flowerpot.

"There's a lead pastor!"

I let that twist sit in silence for a moment. At the time of this sermon, our congregation had been in an interim situation for over eighteen months. Our beloved lead pastor had to resign unexpectedly for medical reasons, and we have been grieving and looking for a new lead for a very long time.

"But that's not how it works. Watch this."

I click the button and a thirty-second video clip plays, showing a time-lapse film of a bean growing roots underground for seven days before the sprout reaches the surface.

"Wasn't that video cool? This is how the kingdom of Heaven works. Did you notice that it took seven days before the sprout broke the surface? Yet even this video isn't that helpful, because it is a sort of magic in itself. We watched it in thirty seconds. If we really watched it, we would have to stand here *for seven days* before anything visible happens!"

> *I click the button one last time. A slide appears that says,* "It is a *mystery*, not magic."
>
> "This is what I needed to hear this week," *I continue.* "God is at work, all the time, but often it is work that happens below the surface, apart from anything that we can do. All we can do is trust that God is faithful to God's promises. Eventually the harvest will come.
>
> "You are raising children.
>
> "You are waiting for something to happen.
>
> "We are waiting for a new lead pastor. It will happen, in God's time. The kingdom of God is at hand. Do we see it? Do we trust it?"

Allow me to explain the structure behind this visual sermon. A wise preacher told me once, when I was beginning my preaching career, that a good sermon should always land where it took off. This is also called bookending a sermon. I began with the visual of the flowerpot on the stage. That was a visual cue to the congregation that something was going to happen related to planting. I opened with a story about Harry Potter and magic. These seemed unrelated to the parable throughout most of the sermon. This tension was intended to keep people wondering, "How will this talk about four soils connect to Harry Potter and magic?" The twist was that there is no magic, only mystery.

The point of my sermon was to embrace the slow, hidden, and often frustrating nature of the kingdom of God. I could have just stated at the beginning, "The kingdom of God is a slow, frustrating mystery."

Instead, I employed four types of visual elements to draw people into the message and, hopefully, help them see it more clearly.

5

Without Speaking a Word

Two-Dimensional Images

In the previous chapter, we discussed the broad topic of how everything in the worship space is a visual element for preaching, and there are many ways to introduce physical objects into that space to create visual sermons. Images can exist both physically and digitally. Here are some possible places to use an image:

- in the bulletin
- in a printed bulletin insert or handout that people can hold during worship and take home
- on an easel in the narthex so people view it as they enter worship
- on an easel at the front of the worship space
- suspended from the ceiling or hanging on a wall
- projected on a screen

Connecting with Your Visual Arts Community

You don't have to be an artist to create images. Go back to the previous chapter and think about all the physical objects that you might want to introduce to your worship space: tapestry, sculpture, wood carving. There are probably people in your congregation who (a) can create the object themselves or (b) know someone who can. In this chapter, we focus on two-dimensional images—paintings, drawings, photographs, graphic designs. Your congregation likely includes artists, photographers, and graphic designers who would love to be able to use their artistic gifts in worship.

The real challenge for the preacher is how to connect with the arts community. Cyndee Buck is an artist and was the director of visual arts at a large Midwest Lutheran congregation for sixteen years. I sat down with her to pick her brain about how to create a visual arts community that intersects with worship and preaching. She offered one key word: relationships. She also offered some practical advice on how to connect to your arts community and build relationships.

First, a word of caution. Let's be honest. Many times the great brainstorm for a perfect image for Sunday's sermon comes in the late hours of Saturday night. Right? No matter how well you know a local artist, it isn't advisable to call them up at midnight and ask them to whip up an image by 8:00 a.m. You can't be a procrastinator preacher to make these suggestions happen! They take a little planning to work well. Now let's hear what Cyndee has to offer.

Call for Art

Put out a "call for art" around an upcoming worship theme, perhaps the focus of a sermon series or a liturgical season. Artists are often looking for a prompt to ignite their next piece. Think of your call for art like an art show. Publicize the worship theme a month or two in advance and give specifications about the type and scope of work you desire (photographs, painting, graphic design, any combination of media, size limitations, due date, etc.). You might find someone in your congregation who appreciates art and is very organized to be the curator for your art show.

On the day the sermon or sermon series begins, display the art in high-traffic spaces in your building. You might choose one or two pieces to display in the worship space, perhaps rotating through all the pieces that have been submitted as long as the theme or season continues. Depending on the medium of the work, you might include a scan or photograph of the art (or if the work is a photograph, the art itself) in your projected presentation. Or you may choose to not include the art directly in your sermon and simply allow the collection of art in the narthex to be the piece that engages the congregation in the theme of your sermon.

Make sure to do two things when you have the art show: First, have a gallery opening. Set aside a two-hour block of time when you will serve finger food (wine and cheese if your church allows it) and invite the artists and the community to come and enjoy the art for its own sake. Make sure to introduce the artists to one another, in addition to guests. (Gallery openings are a great way to meet people.) Second, create a database of the artists who participate. Your resource list has begun. Be sure to reach out to the artists periodically to see how they are doing in their artistic pursuits.

Form an Art Group

Many congregations have a quilters group and an altar guild. These two groups have often provided visual arts for mainline churches and have been culturally accepted in them. What if you invited a group of visual artists of all types (along with art appreciators) to gather around the topic of art? The group could study how art and worship relate. The congregation could host workshops where artists create together regularly. Guest artists could be invited to present their techniques. The art group might gather regularly to do all of the above over time.

I formed a group like this in one congregation I served. They all knew that I am a visual artist, and I personally wanted to build relationships with other visual artists in the congregation. I invited two artists to be the leaders of the group, then challenged them to reach out to other artists to make personal invitations. The church was named Grace Lutheran, so we called the group The Art of Grace. We met monthly. Each meeting was slightly different but always highlighted one member of the group who shared their work and process. Sometimes we would talk about art topics. Sometimes we created something together. Sometimes we took field trips to paint en plein air (that means to paint outside, from real life). Each year we hosted an art show and invited local high school students to submit work. The narthex was filled with amazing art for a month. These artists often created pieces that would be incorporated into worship and sermons.

Form a Creative Arts Worship Team

The above examples emphasize art and artists for art's sake. It is important to communicate that the preacher is not motivated to encourage artists purely for the exploitation of their art in worship. No one wants to be used for their skills, especially artists.

Another way to celebrate artists' gifts is to invite them to gather with other artists and creative people for the specific purpose of brainstorming around worship and preaching. Imagine what might happen if you gathered a group of artists around the upcoming preaching texts, engaged in Bible study, and brainstormed themes and images. You, as the preacher, might be pleasantly surprised by the direction this group might take your sermons. Additionally, if the artists are invested in the ideas, the chances are they will be more motivated to produce art for a sermon or respond to a wider call for art.

Finding Images

Let's get realistic for a moment. As much as you would love to build an artist community as described above, there are two harsh realities: (1) it takes a lot of time and energy, and (2) sometimes—more often than not—you think of an image for your sermon in the final hour. You are on your own. So how do you find the perfect image for your sermon?

I posted this question on the Visual Preacher Facebook group: "Where do you find images for your sermon?" One of my colleagues responded, in her usual lovingly sarcastic way, "Google, Steve . . . Google." I could hear the implied "Duh!" at the end of the sentence.

Yes, many of us have become trained to pick up our mobile device; say, "Hey, Siri" (or whatever artificial intelligence you have at your fingertips); and ask whatever question comes to mind in that moment. Never before have humans had such ready access to so much information . . . and so many images.

I encourage you to use a web search engine to find images. It is fast and there are millions of images on the web. Type a topic, narrow your search to "image," hit enter, and you will be overwhelmed. The images you see will probably be stunning, and they may even prompt you to think about your sermon in a different way. You will be tempted to right-click and save the image to your hard drive and pop it into your PowerPoint right away.

But listen to me carefully: *proceed with caution*. The use of images that are copyrighted is a tricky quagmire of legal ambiguity for preachers. It is best practice to assume that every image you find on the internet is copyright protected unless otherwise specifically noted. You must gain permission from the creator in order to use an image. Only if you see a specific note that the image is available under a Creative Commons license can you use it without specific permission.

Let me state the central principle clearly. *It is illegal* to project an image in your sermon for which you do not have permission to project or reproduce. It really is that simple.

When you search for an image, the easiest way to ensure an image falls under a Creative Commons license is to search Creative Commons websites or to use a photo library service that offers royalty-free stock photographs. You also have the option to pay for images or subscribe to a stock-image service to gain access to the photos you desire. There are many sites on the internet and the list will most certainly change over the years. I currently go to Unsplash.com first.

Searching for images is not difficult. I recently preached on Genesis 15:1–6. God leads Abram out under the night sky and says, "Count the stars. . . ." I went to Unsplash.com and typed "stars" in the search bar. The search results offered a collection of beautiful star fields. I chose one and downloaded it. The photographer gave permission in the download to use the photo. He also asked to have his name displayed to give him credit. Any time I used that photo in my PowerPoint presentation, I pasted "photo by" and typed his name. I could feel confident that this image was legal as I used it in my sermon.

Crowdsourcing Images

Another free, fun method to obtain images and stories for your sermon is crowdsourcing. It is a process in which a creator—in this case, the preacher—includes the audience in thinking about, creating, and contributing to the solution for a problem. The idea is to get as many people as possible to contribute something small and simple. When many people do something small, the aggregate effect can be something grand.

The advent of social media has made crowdsourcing fast and widely accessible. Crowdsourcing on social media is similar to the process of creating an artist group and promoting a "Call for Artwork," as discussed above, but there are two significant differences. First, it is not necessarily a call for artists or people who would consider themselves artists. It is a call for photos that anyone can take on their smartphone and upload to social media. The submission might be a work of art, a selfie taken at a corner gas station, or a story written in text. It just depends on the topic. The second difference is that it is quick. People can read a call for images on social media and instantly respond. You might even get something from crowdsourcing if you put out a call the day before you preach!

Crowdsourcing for sermons is fun. Here's how it works. Place an announcement on your own or your congregation's various social media platforms a few weeks before a sermon series begins. Again, this is similar to the Call for Art, but it emphasizes that everyone is welcome to participate. It can be a call for photos, for stories that paint a mental picture, or for a combination.

Here's an example. Once I was preaching a series on the book of Job, and I was going to focus a sermon on all the horrible things that Job's so-called friends said to him while he was suffering. Remember those zingers? "Just confess your sin, Job; this suffering is obviously your fault," "Stop being so arrogant and just confess."

The point of my sermon was to help people understand what is appropriate speech and behavior to use when interacting with a person who is experiencing great suffering or grief. This is a heavy subject, so I thought I would lighten it a little by crowdsourcing. I put a message on my Facebook feed asking people to share with me the worst thing anyone said to them when they were experiencing grief or trauma.

Wow! I got some startling examples. I created a series of slides that had the quotes in word balloons like we see when scrolling down a text feed on a phone. The fact that these quotes came from people within the congregation within the previous two weeks gave the statements enormous impact. We were all sharing our own experiences of pain, and it made the burden a little lighter.

That example isn't about crowdsourcing images, but it demonstrates how crowdsourcing works and how the method can be used to gather images. Here's another example. In the summer of 2020, we created a series of family adventures to give our families some activities to do while most of the world was in lockdown due to Covid-19. We created a private group on an app called Band and asked families to take selfies in each location we'd included in the adventure. Sharing these photos created a sense of community and allowed us to talk about community in worship.

Imagine if you were to preach a sermon about the power of daily Bible reading. What if you asked people to take a photo of their Bible and their favorite place to read it and post it to your church's Facebook page? A collage or montage of those images would enhance the sermon immensely by connecting the real spaces in which people read the Bible privately to the real space in which the Bible is being proclaimed publicly.

The possibilities for crowdsourcing images, videos, quotes, and ideas for your sermons are endless in the age of social media. It is important to note, though, that crowdsourcing doesn't have to happen only on social media. You might arrange poster boards in the narthex with a question in big print at the top. Next to the board set up a table with sticky notes and pens. Ask people to share their responses to your prompt. The people in your congregation have a huge amount of insight and life experiences, and they come from diverse contexts almost guaranteed to expand your repertoire of illustrations.

If you want to take crowdsourcing sermons one step further, try asking for real-time input during a sermon. Technology exists to connect a Twitter feed or various other social media platforms to your video projector. Ask a question and get real-time responses in words, images, and text. One such technology is called Mentimeter. You build a presentation on the Mentimeter website. Ask the congregation to take out their mobile devices, go to menti.com on their browser, and enter the code displayed on the screen. As soon as they enter the code, your presentation appears on their device. Whenever you ask a question, they have the opportunity to respond to it on their device, and the responses instantly appear on the screen. This can be used to take polls, take the pulse of the crowd, do a quiz show. It keeps the congregation both visually and kinesthetically engaged throughout the presentation. Be careful to use this type of interaction sparingly. I would recommend that you not allow people to comment throughout the entire sermon. That can be distracting. Only invite the interaction at particular moments when you are trying to make a specific point. The interactions that appear on the screen are the visuals that will make that moment stick in the congregation's memory. They see the image that they are physically creating in real time.

Simple Ways to Create Images

So far in this chapter, we've listed ways that you can get other people to create images for your sermon, or how you can find images online. What if you want to make an image yourself? Fear not! Remember, you don't have to be an artist. An image can be as simple as a stick person or a colored square with text in it.

First, let me show you some methods for creating images. Then I'll wrap up this chapter with some basic design principles to make sure your images look decent.

Presentation Software

You can make some pretty interesting visuals for your sermon without knowing how to draw or purchasing a fancy piece of art software like Adobe Photoshop or Illustrator. Just create it in presentation software. The three most common applications for creating and presenting slides are Microsoft PowerPoint, Apple Keynote, and Google Slides (a free, online option). The chances are that you have one of them on your computer right now. All of these applications are essentially the same, just created by different companies.

What many people don't realize is that these programs are powerful tools for graphic design. Presentation software allows you to add and format text, insert images, and animate images and text, choosing from a myriad of predesigned templates and color schemes, fonts, shapes, and textures. It will not take long to learn the basics of adding text and importing images to your slides. The technology is constantly changing, however, and this book is not a technical manual on how to operate these various software programs. So I encourage you to seek tutorials on YouTube or enroll in a course on a learning site like Lynda.com, Coursera.com, or schoolism.com.

Here's a secret. You don't have to have a video projector to use presentation software to make images for your sermon. Create a slide that you find interesting and helpful for your sermon. Then go to File > Export (or the equivalent command in your software). Choose the file format .jpg and hit save. You can also save slides in various formats like PDF, .png, .mov, and more. Now you have an image that can be printed and placed in your bulletin or displayed on an easel in the front of the worship space.

Online Graphic Design Programs

There are many free online graphic design sites. The two I recommend are Adobe Spark (https://www.adobe.com/express/) and Canva (canva.com). They exist to help those who are not graphic designers make professional quality graphic designs and images very quickly. Both sites offer free accounts and paid accounts; both enable users to create high-quality graphics. Choose colors, fonts, photos, and graphic elements. Choose from premade templates or start from scratch. Mix and match and move the elements around on the screen until you have the stunning image you imagined. Then click save and download. Voila!

Draw, Photograph, Upload

Don't forget, you can always create images IRL (in real life). Take out your crayons, pencils, markers, construction paper. Draw a stick person or make a simple comic strip. If people know you drew it, they won't care about the quality. It will be authentically your voice. Once you've drawn your image IRL, use your phone to snap a picture of it, transfer it to your computer, and insert it into a slide. You might also consider creating images live during your sermon. Take a large flip pad and a marker and write or draw stick people and arrows and diagrams to illustrate your point.

Design Principles

Once you've decided that you want to create an image yourself, you've crossed a major hurdle. You're ready. This final section will offer you a crash course on basic design principles that will help you create excellent images that communicate clearly to your audience.

1. Watch Your Ratios

The term *aspect ratio* refers to the relationship between the width and height of your screen. The two most common aspect ratios are 4:3 (4 units wide by 3 units tall) and 16:9 (16 units wide by 9 units wide). I say units because this is a relative ratio. For example, an image can be 4 inches wide by 3 inches tall or 16 inches wide by 12 inches tall. Both are a 4:3 ratio. Televisions and computer screens of the late twentieth century were built on a 4:3 ratio. The advent of digital video and High Definition Television (HDTV) shifted the standard screen to 16:9, also known as widescreen. Now with the constant evolution of mobile devices, there are no longer any guarantees on the type of screen your viewer will use once your presentation is put online. The preacher who stands inside a building, however, will generally be dealing with either a 16:9 or 4:3 projection system.

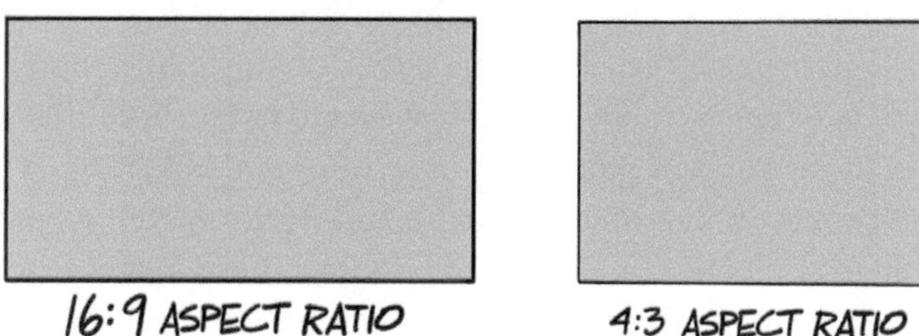

It is important to know what aspect ratio your projection system uses (the "native" aspect ratio) before you design your slides. It is frustrating when you design a presentation at a 4:3 ratio and then discover the system uses 16:9, or vice versa. If you have to shift a completed presentation from one ratio to another, I don't recommend clicking on the "change ratio" button. This will simply convert all your slides to the new ratio and either stretch your composition or squish it to fit the new ratio. This almost never looks good. It is better to open a new presentation that is in the correct ratio and copy the elements from each slide and paste them into the new presentation slide. Then you can adjust the elements into a pleasing composition without any distortion to the text or images. The best practice, though, is always to create your compositions in the native aspect ratio.

2. Less Is More

The worst thing you can do is cram your slide full of small text. First, it is really hard to read. Second, no one will read it. Or, those who do want to read every word on the screen will start reading your slide and stop listening to you.

If you want to make several bullet points in your sermon, don't list them all on the same slide. Use one slide for each point. It is better to lead people through seven slides that let them focus on each point than it is to overwhelm them with seven points on one slide in small print. At the very least, present your points one at a time as you move through them, adding each point as you speak it. This can be accomplished with a simple text animation feature in the software. Presenting the points this way will keep the viewer engaged in your present point and not tempted to read ahead of you.

Use large font (28-point font is the smallest you should ever go) and as few words as possible. Limit your design to two font types—one font for headers and another font for details. Too many font types can become distracting. Make sure there is a strong contrast between the value of the font and the value of the background. Place dark fonts against light backgrounds and light fonts against dark backgrounds. The worst combination is yellow text against a white background (or vice versa). Don't do it!

Remember, the beauty of using digital media is that you are not limited by printing cost. In the old days, you might have wanted to cram as much information on one sheet as you could so you didn't have to use as much paper for your handouts. Digital media are just the opposite. You have a virtually infinite canvas upon which you can lead your listener beautifully through your sermon.

3. White Space Is Good

White space is a term that refers to the empty space on a slide. It doesn't have to be white. It is simply the space around the margins and between elements on the slide. The eye likes to have room between objects on the screen. Designers call this "breathing room." This principle is related to the previous point that less is more. It is OK to place one simple object, either a simple string of text or an image, with lots of white space around it on a slide. Again, you can create as many slides as you need to move through the sermon.

4. Animate with Intention

Let's be honest. The animation feature of presentation software is fun. With one click you can make objects spin and dance on your screen in all sorts of ways. You can even add sound effects! There is a natural tendency to animate everything. Slide in this image, twirl in that text, bounce in each point.

It is fun for you, but it can be distracting for the viewer. I have found that subtle effects like a simple fade are more pleasing to the eye than a fly-in or spin effect. Save these effects for moments in the sermon when you intentionally want to grab attention or startle the congregation. But use them sparingly.

When I teach confirmation students (generally middle schoolers), I insert "student book bombs" into the PowerPoint presentation. These are random explosions where a block of text in a word balloon suddenly zooms large on the screen, accompanied by a loud explosion sound. Everyone in the room jumps, and I crack up. The text in the word balloon gives the pages in the student book where students can read more about the topic at hand. I do this for three reasons: (1) it reminds me to recommend this additional reading, (2) it shakes the students from any possible drifting that may have happened in the last five minutes of my presentation, and (3) it is age appropriate. Middle schoolers love this kind of stuff. I wouldn't recommend it for the senior adult class or the early service! You might have to call 911 during your sermon.

5. Color Matters

Color is a language in itself. Basic color theory tells us that there are three primary colors: magenta (red), yellow, and cyan (blue). This is true for print. The three basic colors for video are red, green, and blue. Mixing these three primary colors, along with white and black, creates all the colors in the rainbow.

I will resist the urge to follow the rabbit down the deep hole of color theory, but I encourage you to do some investigation into the emotional impact of color choices. Here is a simple primer. There are three basic ways to categorize color: temperature, saturation, and value.

Temperature

Red, orange, and yellow are "warm" colors. Our brains associate them with warm things in nature like fire and the sun. Blue, green, and purple are "cool" colors. Our brains associate them with cooler things in nature, like water, grass, and shadow.

Saturation

The saturation, or chroma, of a color ranges from bright, pure colors to dull, muted colors. Imagine that you are observing a colorful landscape in the middle of the day. There are no clouds, and the sun is directly overhead, shining brightly on everything. The reds, yellows, and oranges seem to burn hot. The blues and violets are rich and deep. Everything seems vibrant and pulsing with energy. Dark shadows accentuate the three-dimensional quality of every object.

Now imagine that same scene while dark storm clouds roll in overhead. As the clouds cover the sky, the colors fade. The yellows and reds stop burning. The blues and violets turn gray. The dark shadows dissolve, and everything seems to flatten into dull monotony. You can tell that the objects before you are yellow, red, blue, and violet, yet somehow they all share the same dullness.

When the direct sunlight is obscured by clouds, the colors desaturate. Painters have learned how to simulate the muting of colors with the magic of complimentary colors. Imagine a circle that is ringed with swatches of color, arranged like numbers on a clock. If yellow is at the top, where 12 is on a clock, then the next five colors would be evenly dispersed around the circle in this order: Yellow at 12, orange at 1:30, red at 4:30, purple at 6:00, blue at 7:30, and green at 10:30 (see color wheel illustration). Yellow stands opposite purple. Red stands opposite green. Blue stands opposite orange. If you want to desaturate yellow, mix in a little purple and watch the intensity fade. If you mix equal portions of complementary colors, you end up with a muddy brown. Desaturated colors carry less intensity, while fully saturated colors are bristling with energy.

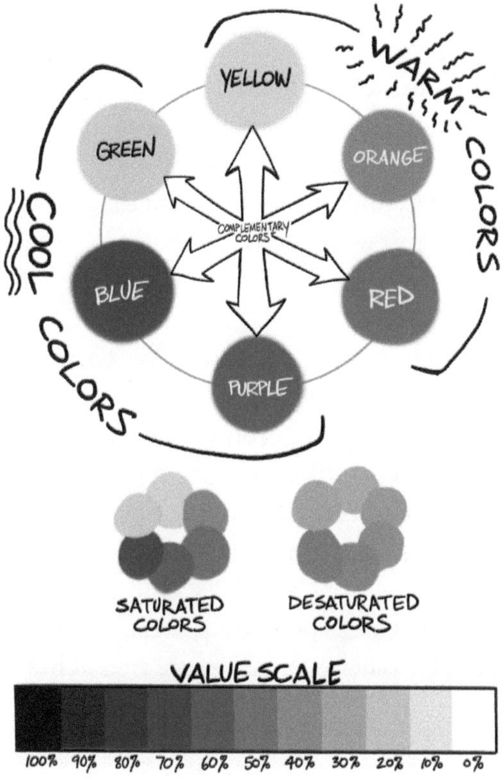

Value

What about white and black? White and black are not colors, they are values. There are two values in color theory: light and dark, also known as tint and shade. The lightest light is white. The darkest dark is black. Mixing white and black makes various shades of gray. When you add white to a color, you create a tint of that color. White turns red into pink and purple into lavender. When you add black to a color, you create a shade of that color. Black turns red into burgundy and purple into, well, dark purple.

So What?

Why does color theory matter for visual preaching? The colors you choose for your slides will subtly influence how your audience receives your message. A bright-yellow background with intense red will burn hot in your viewers' eyes. It is like looking directly into the sun. You can't look at it for long before you need to avert your eyes. You would only use this color combination to punctuate a point you intend to keep on the screen for only a few seconds.

A slide with blues, greens, and purples, on the other hand, will slow your audience down. It will communicate that this is a moment of quiet and peace. You would not want to use this color combination to describe an exciting or intense point.

A slide with tinted colors, also known as pastels, communicates softness. A slide with shades of colors can communicate sternness or gravity. Notice how Good Friday images are usually shades, and Easter ones are pastels. Spend a little time choosing your color palette to make sure it matches the tone of your sermon.

A carefully selected image can communicate powerfully to your audience without you speaking a word. Hopefully this chapter has opened up new pathways to creating helpful images for your sermons. Whether you tap into your artistic community, crowd source, or take the plunge to create your own images, you are only limited by your own imagination for visually enhancing your preaching.

6

Learning a New Language

Videos

So far we have discussed visual preaching in terms of how to use the physical space around us and how to use and create images for our sermons. This final chapter will discuss the use of videos and look at them in two ways. First, we'll talk about how to use video clips that other people have made as visual elements in your sermon. Second, we'll talk about how to create your own videos.

No matter where your videos come from, videos are dynamic. They are inherently multisensory, combining images, movement, and sound. The world has been watching movies and television programming for nearly a century. For most of the twentieth century, moving images were confined to a time and a place. Movies were viewed in the theater. TV programs were viewed on a television at a set time. Now in the digital age, the world is saturated with video, streaming constantly, available on demand to devices of all kinds. The chances are that a vast majority of your congregation watches videos regularly. We watch everything from funny cat videos to deep intellectual teaching to do-it-yourself instructions on cooking and home repairs.

The language of video is quickly becoming an integral part of our vernacular. I believe the visual preacher would benefit greatly from knowing how to use video to speak in a relevant way to the congregation. However, this could be a daunting prospect for many preachers.

"Hey!" you may be thinking, "I didn't go to seminary to be a video producer!"

No, you didn't. But you did go to seminary to learn how to stand in the cultural gap between the text of Scripture and the members of your congregation and the community in which it exists. The preacher would be wise to learn the visual language of video in order to effectively communicate the good news and help people see Jesus.

Why Use Video?

As Covid-19 swept the globe, forcing them to adopt online technology for worship, many preachers learned that video isn't as scary or strange as they thought it might be. Don't get me wrong. There is a significant difference between standing in front of a live congregation to proclaim the gospel and staring at an iPhone on a tripod in your living room. These experiences are worlds apart. Yet they both have their own positives and negatives.

The positives of in-person preaching are numerous. We've stated earlier that preaching is an incarnational act where the preacher embodies the gospel in real space and time. Standing in front of real people, looking into their eyes, seeing their bodies respond to the words and images, feeling the energy in the room, feeling the visceral flow of the Spirit bring unity to a congregation and bond the speaker to the listeners—these are in-the-moment experiences that are impossible to capture through virtual media. Period.

I will never claim that online, virtual, video preaching is superior to in-person, incarnational, community-driven proclamation. Nor will I claim that it is the same experience. I won't even claim that it is "as good as" in-person worship. However, I will claim that the medium of video and the ability to post online have many strengths that in-person preaching does not.

First, online sermons have a wider reach and shelf life. An in-person sermon can have a powerful spiritual impact on the people present, but that is where it stops. No one else can experience that sermon. A video sermon can live online and reach hundreds, thousands, even millions of people across the planet over an indefinite period of time. That potential may horrify some preachers, to be sure. Yet we can never know how the Holy Spirit could use that proclamation in the life of a person on the other side of the planet who needed to hear and see that sermon in their particular moment.

Second, video is the primary medium through which the majority of people assimilate information in the twenty-first century. Even billboards along the highway are now giant video screens. Twenty-first-century brains have been trained to weave together disparate images, text, spoken words, and music into a synthetic and dynamic flow of data. Video communicates on multiple levels in ways that the spoken word alone cannot. If preachers don't utilize this medium well, we may be missing a huge opportunity to reach our audience simply because we are not speaking the vernacular.

Third, the medium of video is a wonderful opportunity to craft sermons that will capture the listener's imagination. Preachers have always had to adapt to their context and embrace the media available to them. The options have been limited for centuries, however. Most preachers have had few choices: stand in the pulpit, or walk outside it and move around the chancel? The twentieth century and the invention of electronic audio amplification (microphones) transformed how preachers preach. Suddenly the preacher did not have to project loudly to be heard in the back of the room. The timbre of the preacher's voice could become more intimate. Slide projectors allowed preachers to project full-color images on a screen. The invention of video projection has allowed preachers to easily incorporate moving images into the experience of the sermon. A close-up of a bee pollinating a flower embodies the wonders of God's creation. A panoramic sweep of a lake, mountain range, or forest helps listeners calm their restless minds and bodies and listen for the promptings of the Spirit. A collage of groups gathered for meals illustrates the gifts of community.

Perhaps the most significant feature of using video as the primary medium to deliver a sermon—one many preachers miss—is that you do not have to point a camera at a pulpit and preach as if you were preaching to a room of people.

Think about that for a minute.

There is no one in the room. Why stand at a pulpit and pretend that people are there? The viewing audience is anywhere and everywhere. The great irony of video is that while it does not create an immediate personal connection, it is far more intimate than in-person preaching. Each viewer can have a one-on-one experience with the preacher. The preacher can be as close to the camera or as far away as the particular sentence being spoken predicates. You, as the preacher, can imagine yourself having a conversation with each member of your congregation, individually, at a coffee shop, and conveying your thoughts directly to their heart and mind.

Embrace the medium.

Preaching Live versus Preaching on Video

One way to understand the difference between preaching live and preaching for video is to imagine yourself in a theater watching a musical performance. You are there in the moment. The actors and musicians are physically present, and the story unfolds before you in real time. Anything could happen. Someone could trip. An entrance could be missed.

Live performance is exciting, but it is also very limited. You are fixed in your seat. You are a certain distance from the stage. You can never see the actors up close. There is always a distance and a barrier between the audience and the performance. The sets are limited because they are confined within one stage and there is a small window of time to change sets and costumes. Stage performers must project their voices and make large movements in order to be seen by everyone in the room. Stage acting is not like real-life human behavior.

Storytelling on film is radically different from the live theater. It is far more intimate than the stage. Live theater is about the relationship of the entire stage to the entire crowd. Film can feel one-on-one. The camera becomes the eyes of the single viewer. It can see as wide as a vast landscape, or it can get so close to an actor that you can see the details in her eyes. Film can jump through time and location in the blink of an eye. There are no boundaries. It can be bigger than life, or it can be as subtle as a drop of dew on a single blade of grass.

Preachers have always been trained to preach in a live stage performance mode. Worship happens in real time, in a physical space, and with the preacher speaking to the whole room. When we stand in front of a live audience to preach, a performative act happens in that moment. A synergistic energy is created between the preacher and the congregation. The clock is ticking. There is only one chance to say and do the things you intended to say and do during the sermon. When the sermon is done, it is done. We move on to the next part of the service.

The obvious difference between live preaching and video preaching is that the latter is not in front of a live audience. When a preacher creates a video sermon, they must switch to a filmmaking mindset. You are no longer speaking to a large room full of people. The communication takes place between just you and the viewer. This might be hard to believe because intellectually you know that potentially hundreds of people will watch the video. But this isn't how the video is experienced. Most people will be sitting alone (or with one or two other people) in the comfort of their own private space, having an intimate moment with you on screen.

Embracing the medium of video for preaching entails following a few simple principles. Don't capture your whole body standing behind the pulpit, pretending that you are preaching to a large room; sit down. Frame the camera in a close-up shot that captures just your upper body. Speak to the camera as if you were having coffee with a couple of close friends. That approach will feel more natural on camera than trying to preach the way you do in a room full of people.

Embrace the movie magic the medium affords you. Change locations. Record part of your sermon while you are walking. Choose a physical location that connects to the topic of the sermon. Include graphics and music. Making a sermon as a video is only limited by your imagination and your skill level in movie editing.

A Reminder about the Law

Before we discuss the details of video production, let us revisit the issue of copyright law as it applies to video. A video clip is a piece of intellectual property in the same way that a still image is. I invite you to refer to the previous chapter's sections about how to find images. All of these principles apply directly here. You probably have videographers and editors in your congregation who would love to produce videos for worship and sermons. You can crowdsource videos via social media as easily as crowdsourcing images.

I emphasized this point in the last chapter, but I will revisit it here. *It is illegal to show other people's videos in worship.* It is that simple. The Copyright Act of 1976 forbids the public performance of any copyrighted videos. Videos are meant for private viewing only. You can download and use in worship only videos that are (a) clearly marked with a Creative Commons license, (b) from a subscription site, or (c) used with express written permission from the creator.

The best option for the preacher/congregation that wants to use other people's videos is to purchase a license. The two most common places to purchase a license to show video content are mplc.com and cvli.com. The Motion Picture Licensing Corporation (MPLC) was created for general audiences and services educational institutions, corporations, and all forms of public gathering. Christian Video Licensing International (CVLI) specifically services churches through its Church Video License. Both organizations provide a blanket license that will allow an organization to play a video publicly with no legal ramifications.

Using Professional Videos

Movies and television are the shared narrative of our society. More people are familiar with Star Wars and Harry Potter in our society than they are familiar with the journeys of the apostle Paul or the message of the Hebrew prophets. The shared cultural language of popular stories is a wonderful source for connecting the Scriptural narrative to the cultural narrative. A thirty-second clip from a popular movie or a current event on a newscast can instantly bring the congregation into a shared cultural experience. Sometimes the power of that visual moment, combined with the music and the memory of experiencing the clip for the first time, can be far more powerful than the preacher simply saying, "Do you remember when such-and-such happened in that one movie?"

Along with popular film and television clips, there are several organizations that create rich, visual multimedia content for local congregations to use in worship and preaching. Most publishing houses have a division that offers downloadable content. Each of these websites requires a subscription membership that allows the user to download content and provides licenses to display it publicly. More sites are being created every day. You will need to determine which organization aligns most closely with your own theological orientation before you commit to a subscription. Refer to the appendix for a list of resources.

How to Make a Good Video

Preachers might create two types of videos. The first type is the clip used within a sermon. For example, let's say you are going to preach on the text in Luke 24, when Jesus is walking on the road to Emmaus with two disciples. You might want to show a video clip of three people walking on a path. You could easily make that video with your phone. When you use your own video clips, you don't have to have a license to use them because you made them.

The second type of video is one where you record your entire sermon as a video and post it on various social media platforms to offer a wider range of people access to your sermon. This type of video production has become more common among preachers since the Covid-19 pandemic. Most of the practical tips I offer in this section will be geared toward this second type of video, but the principles apply to any kind of video production.

Camera or Phone?

The smartphone significantly changed the use of video. Nearly everyone now has a camera with them all the time. The quality of these cameras is staggering. My iPhone takes photographs and videos that match and even exceed the quality of those taken on the expensive digital camera I bought in the early 2000s.

The question, then, is whether the video preacher should invest in an expensive camera or simply record the video on a smartphone. The answer is . . . it depends. The simple answer is that a smartphone video can be as high quality as a video shot with an expensive camera. This is especially true if the subject of the video is a simple close-up of one person talking directly into the camera in a static setting. If you have a smartphone, you can use it without feeling like you are being cheap or cutting corners.

The advantage of an expensive camera is that it has more ability to zoom in and out, focus on specific parts of the frame, and change the depth of field. But unless you plan to have a camera operator and move around during your sermon, you won't need all those extras. Honestly, you won't.

Lighting Matters

Lighting is part of visual grammar. How you light a scene creates the mood of the scene and communicates the tone of the message. Try this experiment. Stand in front of a mirror in a room where you can turn off all the lights and it is dark. Take a flashlight, or the light on your phone, and hold it in different positions in relation to your face.

First, hold it up and to the left of your face. Now hold the light directly above your head and shine it down. Finally, hold the light directly under your face, shining up. How would you describe the three pictures that these lighting scenarios create? Do it a few times and notice the differences.

The first lighting scenario is known as a standard setting. Your face probably looks normal to you. It is normal because the human brain is used to seeing faces lit from above and slightly to the front. The sun is above us and shines on our faces. Indoor lights usually hang from the ceiling and spread evenly throughout the room, so the light shines into our faces.

The second lighting scenario may have been unsettling. When a single light shines directly above the head, shadows are cast down into the eyes sockets, obscuring the eyes and shrouding the figure in mystery.

The third scenario may have frightened you. Your top eyelids disappeared in shadows. Your features probably seemed disfigured. You may not have recognized your own reflection.

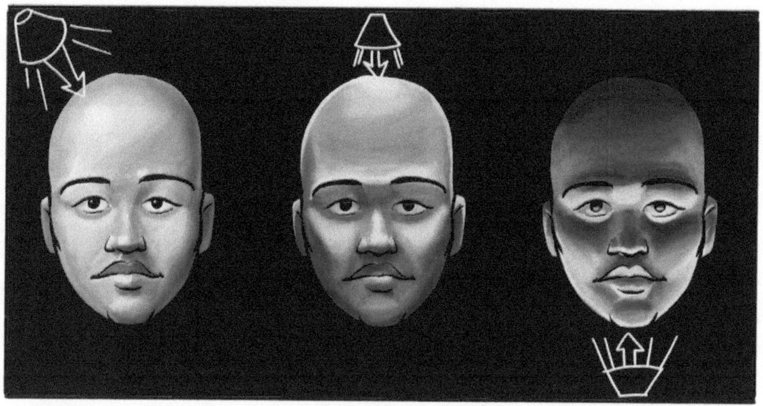

This lighting scenario is considered a horror setting because it inverts our normal expectations and startles us.

It is easy to make lighting mistakes when you are trying to film your own sermon video. Here are three common lighting mistakes.

1. *Horror lighting.* Imagine this scenario. You set up in your office and try to figure out where and how to mount your phone. You prop the phone up on your desk by leaning it against a stack of books. You turn on your desk lamp. If the desk lamp is below your eye level, then you will inadvertently paint your video with a horror tone. Don't do that. You really don't want to scare your listeners . . . unless you do. Then hold light directly under your chin and cackle.

2. *Back lighting.* Pay attention to the light behind you. In the middle of the day, a window in the background will often overpower your camera. The camera sees all that light and then obscures your face into a silhouette.

Unless you are going for the "anonymous witness" effect, make sure you aren't backlit.

3. *Top lighting.* Many rooms have a single light in the center of the ceiling. It is easy to think that simply turning on that overhead light will be sufficient to illuminate your shot. If the light is directly above your head, your eyes will disappear and you will come across as a little bit creepy, no matter how nice your tone of voice may be.

Lighting Setups: Good, Better, Best

Now that you have been horrified by all the possible lighting mistakes one can make, we must ask the question: How do I achieve good lighting? Three basic lighting setups are acceptable: one-point, two-point, and three-point. They are all good, but some are better than others. Your choice of lighting setups will depend on both time and budget constraints.

1. *One-point lighting is good.* If you have only one light source, use it correctly. Always, always, always place that light source slightly above your head and to one side, at a forty-five- to sixty-degree angle from the center line of your face. In other words, imagine that your face is in the center of a clock. Your eyes are looking at twelve o'clock. Your light should be at either ten or two.

2. *Two-point lighting is better.* Set your first light source in the place described above. The second light source must be slightly dimmer than the primary light. Place it level with your face and on the opposite side of the primary light. This is known as a fill light, because it fills in the shadows caused by the primary light source.

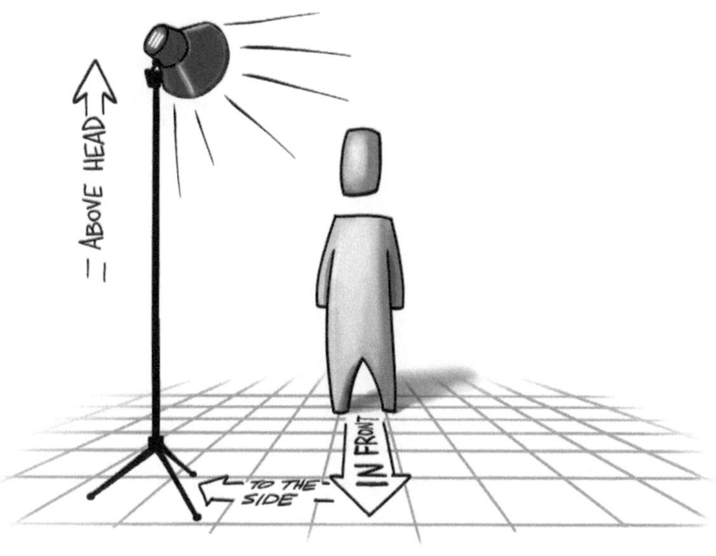

ABOVE HEAD
TO THE
SIDE
IN FRONT

ABOVE HEAD
TO THE
SIDE
IN FRONT

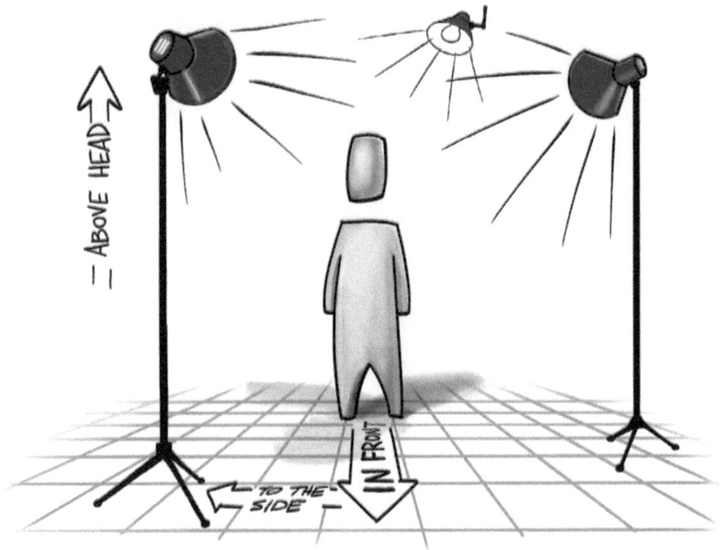

If your secondary light source has the same intensity as your primary light source, there are a few ways that you can lessen the intensity of the secondary source. First, if you are near a wall, point the light (or tip the shade) toward the wall and let the light bounce off the wall and fill the shadows. Second, you can cover the light with a white cloth. Be sure to not lay the cloth directly on a light bulb. This can cause fires. Third, if the wall doesn't work, position a piece of white paper or foam board near your face. It will reflect the primary light and bounce it softly back to your face.

3. *Three-point lighting is best.* Place the first two lights just like you would in two-point lighting. Then add a third light above and behind your head. This creates a rim of light around the top of your head and shoulders. This is especially nice if you are in front

of a dark background. The rim lighting helps the viewer recognize the form, rather than losing it in the background.

Many one-, two-, and three-point lighting kits are available online. The lights often come in a "soft box," a flexible box that encloses the bulb and directs the light forward. The box can be covered by a scrim, a translucent white fabric that softens the light. The softening reduces harsh reflections on the skin.

Composition Basics

A video screen is a horizontal rectangle. Always keep that in mind. The term "composition" refers to how the elements—objects, shapes, lines, text, and so forth—are arranged within the rectangle.

To understand the principles of composition, first imagine a grid on our screen. When you look at the rectangular frame of your video, draw imaginary lines across the screen. Begin with three vertical lines. The first vertical line runs down the middle of the screen and splits the field into two halves: left side and right side. The next two vertical lines are at the one-third mark. They divide the screen into three equal sections.

Then draw or imagine three horizontal lines, similar to the vertical lines. The first line runs through the center of the frame, intersecting the center vertical line and defining the exact center of the frame. The other two lines divide the frame into three equal sections from top to bottom.

You now have two overlapping grids. The first grid forms a quadrant, marked by the intersecting center lines. The second grid has nine sections, marked by the four one-third dividing lines. If you want to take your grid to the next level, draw two diagonal lines. The first connects the upper left corner to the bottom right corner. The second connects the bottom left corner with the upper right corner. These two lines form an "X" and intersect at the center point with the vertical and horizontal lines.

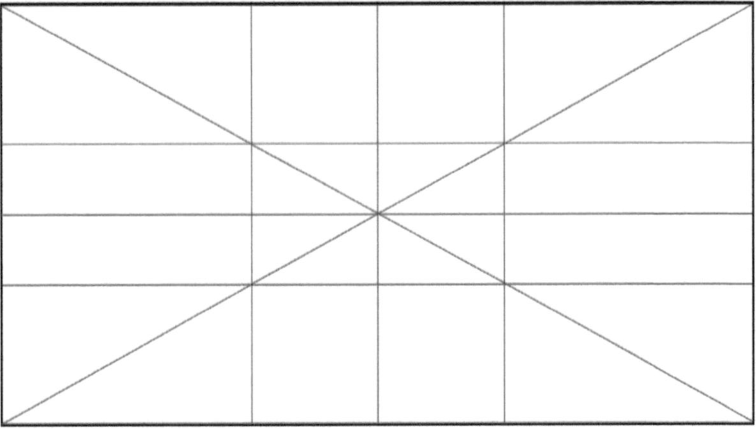

Most likely, the majority of the videos you produce for your sermons will be simple, talking-head videos. That means you will have one camera pointed directly at your face. The camera will not move during the sermon, and your body will stay in the same spot. Notice that I didn't say your body will not move. You need to move a little. Make motions with your hands. Lean in. Smile. The worst thing you can do is stay rigid like a statue while recording a talking-head video. You might as well offer a sound recording and skip the video altogether.

Direct Address

Two basic compositions work well for talking-head videos. The first is the symmetrical, direct address. Your body should be parallel to the plane of the camera lens. In other words, you are facing the camera directly, shoulders square. If you do not have a camera operator (which you probably won't), be sure that your phone or camera allows you to view yourself while you are in front of the camera. Most smartphones have a front-facing camera. If you are using a video camera, use one that allows you to flip the view screen forward, so you can see the shot while you are in it.

This symmetrical, direct-address composition requires three things:

- First, position your face so the vertical center line runs down the middle of your nose.
- Second, line up your eyes with the top horizontal one-third line.
- Third, make sure your chin does not go below the bottom one-third line.

You can play with this third point. Zoom your camera in and out until the size of your head feels comfortable in the frame. Always position your eyes on the top one-third line, and

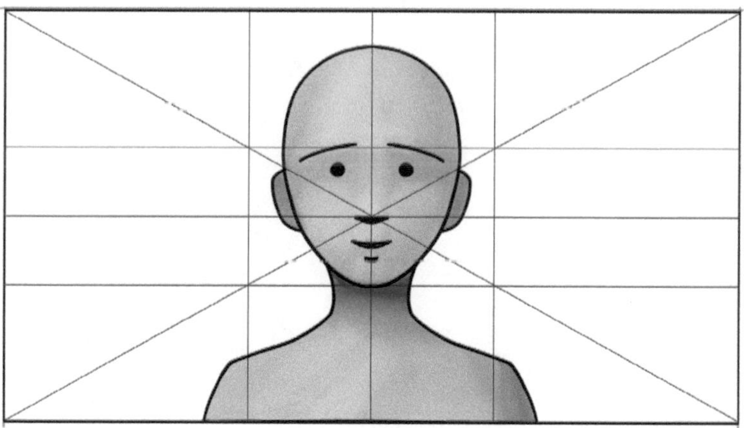

never make your chin go lower than the bottom one-third line. If you exceed these guidelines, the close-up will be too extreme and make people uncomfortable. It is equivalent to standing directly in front of a person and facing them on an elevator. Don't do it.

Three-Quarter Composition

The second basic talking-head composition is the three-quarter view. Position your body at a forty-five-degree angle from the camera. When you look directly at the camera, your head will be turned. This composition requires "looking space" on the side of the screen that your body is facing. The way to achieve this is to align the center of your body on one of the side one-third lines. If your body is turned slightly to the left (as viewed on the screen), then align your body with the right side one-third line. This will allow "looking space" to the left of the screen. Your back will be toward the right side of the screen. If your body is turned slightly to the right, do just the opposite. Align your body on the left vertical one-third line.

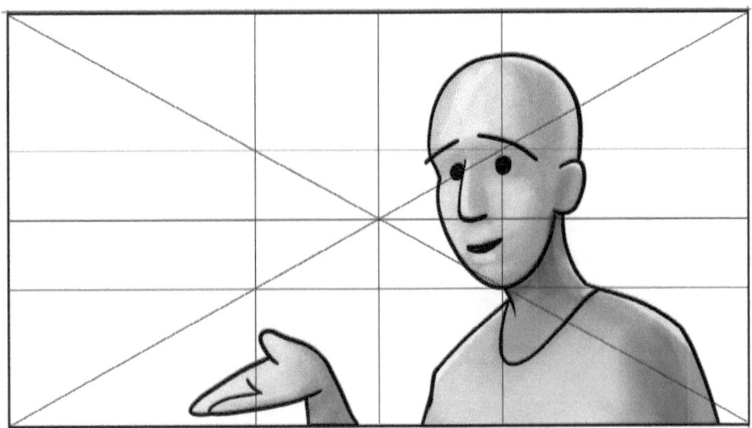

It is important to follow the same eye and chin rules as the direct-address composition. Always keep your eyes on the top horizontal one-third line, and never let your chin go below the bottom horizontal one-third line. This composition may feel more natural if you show more of your upper body in the shot, so your chin may not even go lower than the horizontal center line.

Choosing the Composition

How do you choose between these two compositions? Which is better?

For the most part, this is a matter of taste. If you want to address your audience simply, with no visuals other than your talking head, then choose the direct address.

The three-quarter composition allows for more flexibility in your sermon. Opening up the looking space on one side of the screen allows you to fill that space with something. You may want to sit in front of a fireplace and have a "fireside chat" feel for your sermon, placing the fireplace in the looking space. You may want to include a beautiful painting or a floral arrangement in the looking space to make the setting more aesthetically pleasing.

The looking space also allows room for you to hold up objects during the sermon. If you read text during your sermon, it feels nicer to the viewer if they can see the book in your hand as you look down into the looking space. This seems more natural than looking down and off-screen in the symmetrical composition.

If you have the ability to do postproduction editing and are able to bring graphics into your composition, you will definitely want to leave looking space for them.

Experiment with these two basic compositions. The important thing to keep in mind is the alignment of your eyes and the size of your head. It is very off-putting to the viewer to have a talking head that is too low on the screen or too far to one side or way too big.

There is one more point we must address before leaving the topic of composition. Be conscious of the angle of your camera. Never position the camera lower than your eyes. This angle places the viewer beneath you. This angle is used in cinematography to communicate dominance in the character. Unless you want to seem like you are lording it over your congregation, don't do it.

It is OK if the camera is slightly higher than your eyes. This will cause you to look up slightly. This angle portrays a sense of innocence or submission. It also hides the double chin a little more!

The best angle is to have the camera even with your eyes. It places the viewer on equal terms with you and feels more natural.

Also be aware of the vertical and horizontal lines in your environments. If you are sitting in front of an object that has strong vertical lines, like a bookcase or the corner of a wall, be sure that those vertical lines are parallel with the vertical edges of your frame. The horizontal lines are most important in the symmetrical direct-address composition. Make sure the horizontals are parallel, or you will lose the symmetry of the composition. The three-quarter composition allows more flexibility with horizontal lines, since your body is turned away from the camera. Little things like these lines not being parallel can be distracting to the viewer.

Background

Pay attention to your background. The viewer will notice everything. This is especially true if the camera stays fixed in one spot for the entire sermon.

Once I was recording a Facebook Live video from my back patio. It was during the early days of the Covid-19 pandemic and shortly after the murder of George Floyd and the ensuing protests. Everyone was on edge. I created weekly Facebook Live videos during the pandemic as an attempt to create a connection point for the congregation while everyone was sheltering in place to subdue the spread of the virus.

I was sitting at my patio table. I had made sure that my composition was right, following the rules of the previous section. My background was filled with mostly the side of my house. The far right third showed some grass and part of our flower bed.

I hit "Go Live" and started talking. A few minutes into the broadcast, our dog started wandering around in the grass, in my shot. Remember, this is a live broadcast, and I'm talking about serious things that are going on in the world. Yet while I'm talking, I'm having a conversation with myself: "What happens if the dog does his business right there, on camera?!"

Thankfully, he did not. I found out later, however, that many of my viewers were distracted by the dog and were asking themselves the same question!

The moral of this story: make sure you are aware of everything that is in your background before you hit record. During the pandemic, many of us became used to seeing people framed in rectangles on live video. We got used to the fact that most of the videos were poorly framed and poorly lit. But be honest, how many times were you distracted by objects in the speaker's room and found it hard to listen to what they were trying to communicate?

Don't let that happen with your video sermons. Be intentional with every object. Remember, less is more!

Sound

Video is a multisensory experience, and the audio component of video is as important as the visual. Most preachers don't have a budget, the staff, or the experience to do fancy things with sound, such as adding music or sound effects and enhancing the audio quality. Don't worry. It's OK.

Here are some simple tips to help ensure that you have solid audio quality.

First, record in a quiet space. Check the room for buzzing lights, a loud furnace vent, traffic noise from outside, other people in the building. The quieter, the better.

Second, get a microphone. Most smartphones and video cameras have a microphone built in. These microphones, especially the ones in phones, are designed primarily for a speaker who is very close to the microphone. When you record a talking-head video for a sermon, you will be slightly too far from the microphone to get clear, crisp audio. The microphone picks up too much ambient noise, and you can sound like you are speaking inside a tin can.

The simple solution is to get an external microphone. Many lavalier microphones on the market are designed for the smartphone and plug directly into the phone. Be aware that not all phones have the same connections. The most important thing to keep in mind is to ensure that the connections on the microphone you purchase are designed for the device on which you record, or that you also purchase the necessary adapter.

These microphones are not expensive. But trust me, they will make a big difference in the quality of your video. I purchased a microphone kit that came with two microphones, two extension cables, and a splitter, which allows me to record two people speaking on microphones at the same time plugged into one phone. This comes in handy for recording interviews. The package cost less than thirty dollars.

Editing

I first studied filmmaking in the late 1980s. We actually shot movies on film and had to have it developed at a shop. The process of making a movie was to physically scroll through hundreds of feet of film and literally cut the film apart and splice various parts together with Scotch tape.

Thank the Lord for digital film and nonlinear editing.

You may be trembling with anxiety right now at the thought of editing film. "I don't know the first thing about editing," you think. "I have no technical skills in this area." Don't worry. You really don't have to know much.

Basic Editing

The most basic form of editing is called trimming. Most smartphones and computer video applications have a feature called "Trim." This allows you to clip the beginning and ending off your videos with a simple step.

Trimming is a necessary feature when you record your own video. Here's why. When you press the "Record" button on your device, it will capture you moving away from the camera and getting into position. Then when you are finished with your sermon, it will record you leaning forward or walking to the camera to hit the "Stop" button.

You don't want the reaching portions of your video to be the first and last thing your viewers see.

Follow this simple procedure:

- Press the record button and get situated in the frame. Take your time to make sure the composition is correct.
- Hold up your hand and display five fingers. Count down, speaking the words "five, four . . ."
- At the word "three," don't verbalize the word, but say it in your mind and put your hand down.
- When you reach "one" in your mind, begin your sermon.
- When you are done with your sermon, stay still and count to five in your mind.
- Then reach forward and hit the "Stop" button.
- As soon as you are done recording, take the microphone out of the connector and play the video back. Make sure it looks good and sounds good. If everything is fine, then press the "Edit" button and trim your video at the front and back. You will have visual clues. Trim it at the beginning to just past the point when you put your hand down. Trim it at the end of the video to just before you lean forward.

Following these simple guidelines will ensure that you have clear, clean space at the beginning and end of your video.

Advanced Editing

The ability to edit a video in editing software opens up many possibilities for the preacher. First, it releases the preacher from the pressure to get everything right the first time. Knowing that you have the opportunity to edit after the recording session allows you to stop midsermon, go back, and start over. You can edit out the bad parts later. It also opens up the possibility of seamlessly adding elements such as photos, graphics, and other videos into the flow of the sermon.

This book is not a technical guide on how to edit video. You can learn to edit by watching YouTube tutorials or tutorials built into your video editing software of choice. Or you can work with a video editor in your congregation or staff to edit the sermon for you. (Keep in mind that the more people you have involved in the process, the further in advance you will need to create your video.) But let me offer some things that you can do with video editing software that might encourage you to experiment.

1. *Add graphics.* Editing software lets you import graphics and lay them over your video while the audio plays underneath. This simulates displaying a slide on the screen in a live service while you continue preaching. The viewer is focused on your image while they continue to hear your words.

2. *Combine multiple videos.* You might preach different parts of your sermon from different locations and then splice them together. You might interview different people and combine them into one video. You might include clips from others' videos in your own.

3. *Add music.* Editing software allows you to add multiple layers of sound to a video. You might want an intro jingle or a dramatic chord played at a certain moment or fun transitional music between scenes. (A word of caution: Adding background music while you are speaking can make it difficult for listeners to understand what you are saying. Make sure that any background music is soft enough to allow the voice to come through clearly.)

4. *Use a green screen.* Editing software has the ability to do chroma key effects. This effect picks one color and

makes it transparent, thus revealing anything that is behind the video. You see this technique used every night if you watch the weather on your local news station. The meteorologist is standing in front of a bright green screen, and the weather maps are on another layer of the video. If you record your sermon in front of a green screen, you can place any graphic directly behind you. This allows the audience to see you and your graphic simultaneously.

A Real-Life Example

Keith Anderson is a Lutheran Pastor from New Jersey who is very good at using visuals in preaching. He told me a story about how he used video in a sermon that you might find informative and encouraging.

The sermon was for confirmation Sunday, and he wanted to make an analogy with learning to ride a bicycle—that confirmation is like taking the training wheels off our faith. His youngest child had recently accomplished this great feat, and Keith captured it on his iPhone. His son majestically pedaled his first spins of freedom while Keith ran behind him, capturing a jiggling image and recording the voices of his older children cheering on the young champion.

Keith had options for this sermon.

A. He could simply talk about how confirmation is like taking training wheels off a bike.
B. He could bring in a training wheel and hold it up or put it on a stand next to the pulpit while he talked about the metaphor.

C. He could project a photograph of his son riding without training wheels.

D. He could play the iPhone video clip and let the congregation watch it while he remained silent. Then he could discuss the metaphor.

Keith and I discussed the pros and cons of showing an iPhone video clip like his. Granted, it is possible to get excellent quality video on an iPhone. However, Keith admitted that his clip was about the worst kind of iPhone video you can get. It was in a vertical format, it jostled all around as he ran after his son, and the lighting was horrible.

The poor quality was a definite con. Some people have the expectation that preaching must be excellent or not happen. A video like Keith's would have failed the excellence test and offended the video purist.

There are two significant pros for a video like this, however. First, this is the kind of video that nearly every parent or grandparent with a smartphone has in their photo gallery. It is a "slice of life" video that connects with the congregation's lived experience.

Second, a clip like this allows the congregation to experience the event with all the sights and sounds. You can see the jubilance on the champion's face. You can hear the love in the cheering siblings. You can hear the footsteps of the proud father chasing after his son.

Keith could have told the story with mere words. He is a good storyteller, so that would have been sufficient. He could have told the story with a still photo and that would have enhanced the story slightly. Yet it would have taken him several minutes to tell the story in order to capture the emotion he hoped to communicate.

The clip lasted less than thirty seconds. In those few seconds of sights, sounds, and movement, the congregation physically experienced far more than Keith's words could have ever accomplished.

In case you're curious, Keith chose option E, all of the above. He brought in a training wheel. He talked about the metaphor. He showed a picture, and he played the video.

That's a Wrap

The phrase "that's a wrap" comes from the filmmaking industry. It means the scene is finished and everyone can start packing up for the day. We've come to the end of this chapter on video. You might be overwhelmed. That's OK. You don't have to use video to be a visual preacher. There are many types of videos and many ways to make videos. There really are no wrong ways to use video as a visual element of your sermon. (Except for using them illegally. Don't do that. Get a license.)

If you have never used video, then start small. Purchase a video from a trusted worship shop, like The Work of the People, and show it in your sermon. Ask your congregation how it felt for them. Receive their feedback with openness and grace. Then try again.

You can do it.

NOTES

1: We Wish to See Jesus

1 Dave Daubert, *The Incarnational Preacher* (n.p.: ELCA, 2020), 4, https://download.elca.org/ELCA%20Resource%20Repository/The _Incarnational_Preacher.pdf.
2 SteveThomason, "Interview with Karoline Lewis," YouTube, February 7, 2020, https://www.youtube.com/watch?v=LfCNR6rKe-0.
3 I am thankful to Karoline Lewis for this quote.
4 Richard Jensen, "Thinking in Picture," *Dialog* 43, no. 4 (Winter 2004): 303.

4: Everything Communicates

1 "Turn toward the Light," Metanoia, December 28, 2019, https://www.metanoia.org/light.htm.
2 The current sermon series we are preaching follows the Narrative Lectionary through the Gospel of Mark. I committed myself to illustrating one graphic novel-style page for each text of the series. A new installation of the graphic novel is printed each week.

RECOMMENDED RESOURCES

Books and Articles

Blackwood, Rick. *The Power of Multisensory Preaching and Teaching: Increase Attention, Comprehension, and Retention.* Zondervan, 2013.
This book chronicles Blackwood's DMin thesis project, in which he ran experiments with his congregation to see how multisensory preaching impacted learning and retention. He provides great science behind multisensory communication and learning.

Chaplin, Michael. "From Sticky Note to Storyboard: Developing and Evaluating Ideas." National Public Radio Incubation Lab, May 1, 2019. https://medium.com/public-radio-incubation-lab/ from-sticky-note-to-storyboard-developing-and-evaluating-ideas -8553ba936f52.
This article offers helpful ways to use sticky notes in the brainstorming process.

Duarte, Nancy. *Resonate: Present Visual Stories That Transform Audiences.* John Wiley, 2010.

———. *Slide:ology: The Art and Science of Creating Great Presentations.* O'Reilly Media, 2008.
This trilogy of books provides practical tips on how to create compelling slides in presentation software.

Duarte, Nancy, and Patti Sanchez. *Illuminate: Ignite Change through Speeches, Stories, Ceremonies, and Symbols*. Portfolio, 2016.

"How to Make a Storyboard with Post-Its." Post-it, February 14, 2017. https://www.post-it.com/3M/en_US/post-it/ideas/articles/how-to-make-a-storyboard-with-post-it-products/.

This article offers a really practical process for using sticky notes to make storyboards.

Jensen, Richard. *Envisioning the Word: The Use of Visual Images in Preaching*. Fortress, 2005.

Jensen brings the power of visual communication into dialogue with the Lutheran/Mainline context and tradition of preaching. He makes a compelling biblical, theological, and pedagogical case for why visuals are essential for the proclamation of the gospel.

———. "Thinking in Picture." *Dialog* 43, no. 4 (Winter 2004): 297–303.

Jensen provides a theological framework for why visual communication is essential for effective communication.

Jonker, Peter. *Preaching in Picture: Using Images for Sermons That Connect*. Abingdon, 2015.

A simple and practical approach to using visuals effectively in preaching.

Pollard, Tim. *The Compelling Communicator: Mastering the Art and Science of Exceptional Presentation Design*. Conder House, 2016.

This book provides the scientific framework for why visual presentations are effective tools for communication.

Reynolds, Garr. "Design Tips." Garrreynolds.com, accessed January 7, 2022. https://www.garrreynolds.com/design-tips.

———. *Presentation Zen: Simple Ideas on Presentation Design and Delivery*. New Riders, 2011.

Garr is one of the gurus of visual communication. This book and the accompanying website are full of helpful, practical tips and strategies for effective visual communication.

Shekar, Shruti. "Visual Expression: The 8 Basic Ways to Frame Shots in Your Videos." EnvantoTuts+, September 27, 2015. https://

photography.tutsplus.com/tutorials/visual-expression-the-8-basic
-ways-to-frame-shots-in-your-videos--cms-24641.

> This article will give you the vocabulary to discuss various ways to frame a shot in video. This is a helpful thing to know when working with a team and brainstorming a video project.

Sicinski, Adam. "The Complete Guide on How to Mind Map for Beginners." IQ Matrix, accessed January 7, 2022. https://blog .iqmatrix.com/how-to-mind-map.

> A helpful primer on how to create mind maps and various applications for using them.

Tufte, Edward. *Beautiful Evidence.* Graphics, 2006.

> Tufte dives into the theory and philosophy behind visual communication.

Vyond. "What Is a Storyboard and Why Do You Need One?" January 11, 2021. https://www.vyond.com/resources/what-is-a -storyboard-and-why-do-you-need-one/.

> A helpful article to learn the basics of storyboarding.

Websites

Art in the Christian Tradition. 2007. https://diglib.library.vanderbilt .edu/act-search.pl.

> This is a library of Christian art that is available to use in public presentations.

Christian Video Licensing International. "Church Video License." Accessed January 7, 2022. https://us.cvli.com/.

> The Church Video License is one of the most cost-effective and convenient ways for churches and other ministry organizations to protect themselves from the possibility of being fined for illegal use of videos. The license provides a comprehensive copyright compliance solution.

Mackie, Tim, and John Collins. "BibleProject." Accessed January 7, 2022. www.bibleproject.com.

BibleProject is a crowdfunded, nonprofit animation studio that seeks to create visual resources that help people see that the Bible is a unified story that leads to Jesus. All the resources are free.

MPLC Licensing. Accessed January 7, 2022. https://www.mplc.org/.

This is the place to acquire the necessary license to present videos in front of a large crowd in a public setting.

Thomason, Steve. "A Cartoonist's Guide to the Bible." Accessed January 7, 2022. www.cartoonistbible.com.

This is my website. It is an ever-expanding library of visual resources for the Bible student, teacher, and preacher. It offers downloadable PowerPoints, Image Packs, and PDFs that can be used for your own preaching and teaching.

Unsplash. Accessed January 7, 2022. https://unsplash.com/.

This is my go-to source for royalty-free images.

Working Preacher Books is a partnership between Luther Seminary, WorkingPreacher.org, and Fortress Press.

Books in the Series

Preaching from the Old Testament by Walter Brueggemann

Leading with the Sermon: Preaching as Leadership by William H. Willimon

The Gospel People Don't Want to Hear: Preaching Challenging Messages by Lisa Cressman

A Lay Preacher's Guide: How to Craft a Faithful Sermon by Karoline M. Lewis

Preaching Jeremiah: Announcing God's Restorative Passion by Walter Brueggemann

Preaching the Headlines: Possibilities and Pitfalls by Lisa L. Thompson

Honest to God Preaching: Talking Sin, Suffering, and Violence by Brent A. Strawn

Writing for the Ear, Preaching from the Heart by Donna Giver-Johnston

The Peoples' Sermon: Preaching as a Ministry of the Whole Congregation by Shauna K. Hannan

Real People, Real Faith: Preaching Biblical Characters by Cindy Halvorson

The Visual Preacher: Proclaiming an Embodied Word by Steve Thomason

Forthcoming

Divine Laughter: Preaching and the Serious Business of Humor by Karl N. Jacobson and Rolf A. Jacobson

For Every Matter under Heaven: Preaching on Special Occasions by Beverly Zink-Sawyer and Donna Giver-Johnston

Praise for *The Visual Preacher*

"Information, illustration, inspiration! *The Visual Preacher* provides background and excellent suggestions for preachers to become more visually aware. Steve Thomason offers many helpful practical suggestions, but more importantly, his book will spark creativity in proclaiming the gospel in a way that engages all the senses."

—Mark G. Vitalis Hoffman, Glatfelter Professor of Biblical Studies, United Lutheran Seminary, Gettysburg and Philadelphia, Pennsylvania; ScrollandScreen.com

"As I teach my preaching courses, I see the need for my students to be equipped to engage congregations so they don't merely hear but also see the Scriptures unfold before them. In *The Visual Preacher*, Thomason gives any preacher in any context the tools to unlock that ability. It's a must-have resource I will assign in my courses going forward."

—Stephanie Williams O'Brien, preaching professor, Bethel Seminary, Arden Hills, Minnesota; lead pastor, Mill City Church, Minneapolis; author of *Stay Curious: How Questions and Doubts Can Save Your Faith* (Fortress Press, 2019) and *Make a Move: How to Stop Wavering and Make Decisions in a Disorienting World* (Broadleaf Books, 2021)

"Been wanting to use visuals, but not sure where to begin? *The Visual Preacher* is it! Grounded, relevant, accessible, understandable, immediately applicable. Thomason's many examples give needed, practical direction to help preachers engage people in the Word in today's visual world. A gem for your pastoral library."

—Paul Oman, Drawn to the Word, founder/owner/artist

"*The Visual Preacher* offers encouragement and concrete tips to preachers who are ready to embrace and enhance the visual aspects of proclaiming the good news. Even for those preachers who are not convinced pandemic-induced online preaching is here to stay in one form or another, the book offers guidance for studying the Bible visually, utilizing images and video, and crafting sermons for people who wish to *see* Jesus."

—Shauna K. Hannan, professor of homiletics, Pacific Lutheran Theological Seminary, and core doctoral faculty member, Graduate Theological Union, Berkeley, California

"I've been a fan of Steve Thomason's *Cartoonist's Guide to the Bible* for many years. Now he shows us how we, too, can become visual preachers—even if you're artistically challenged like me!"

—Robert Williamson Jr., professor of religious studies, Hendrix College; author of *The Forgotten Books of the Bible: Recovering the Five Scrolls for Today* (Fortress Press, 2018); cohost of *BibleWorm* podcast

"Wow! I wish you could see me offer that exclamation in person, because the printed word doesn't capture my amazement at what Steve Thomason has accomplished with *The Visual Preacher*. Chock-full of much-needed, practical wisdom from a seasoned preacher, artist extraordinaire, and communication guru, Thomason's book offers the church an incredible and timely gift for all who proclaim the gospel. This little gem is a must for any preacher today."

—Jason Brian Santos, Community Presbyterian Church, Lake City, Colorado